Why Read
the
Bible Through?
&
How Readest
Thou?

Why Read the Bible Through? & How Readest Thou?

Jay P. Green Sr.
J. C. Ryle

Sovereign Grace Publishers, Inc.
P.O. Box 4998
Lafayette, IN 47903

Printed In the United States of America
By Lightning Source, Inc.

WHY READ THE BIBLE THROUGH

by Jay P. Green, Sr.

[All Scripture references are from the *Literal Translation of the Bible*, Revised 1997]

YOU SHOULD READ THE BIBLE THROUGH BECAUSE:

I. Every word and all words of the Scriptures are God's words.

II. God has commanded that you know, read and study the Scriptures.

III. Everything that can be legitimately desired can be sought for and obtained through the Scriptures, including:

    A. Everlasting life

    B. Salvation

    C. Righteousness

    D. Blessedness

    E. Holiness

    F. Purity

    G. Wisdom

    H. Reproof

    I. Satisfaction

    J. Contentment

    K. Freedom

    L. Peace

    M. Joy

    N. Love

    O. Hope

    P. Mercy

    R. Self-control

    S. Comfort and encouragement

    T. Riches, treasure and wealth

    U. Guidance and direction in your life

    V. Full knowledge of the truth (John 14:6)

    W. Safety

    X. Help

    Y. Fruitfulness

    Z. Divine warnings

I. EVERY WORD AND ALL WORDS OF THE SCRIPTURES ARE GOD'S WORDS

"Every Scripture [is] God-breathed and profitable for doctrine, for reproof, for correction, for instruction in righteousness, so that the man of God may be complete, fully furnished for every good work" (2 Timothy 3:16, 17).

"having been born again, not by corruptible seed, but incorruptible, through the living Word of God, and remaining forever. Because all flesh [is] as grass, and all [the] glory of men as [the] flower of grass; the grass was dried, and its flower fell out, but [the] Word of the Lord remains forever. And this is the Word announced as gospel to you" (1 Peter 1:23-25)

A. Is the Bible inspired, or God-breathed?

In his excellent work, *The Inspiration and Authority of the Bible*, B. B. Warfield explains: "The Greek term [θεοπνευτος - θεο = God; πνευτος = breathed] has, however, nothing to say of inspiring or of inspiration: it speaks only of a `spiring' or `spiration' What it says of Scripture is, not that it is `breathed into by God' or is the product of the Divine `inbreathing into its human authors,' but that it is breathed out by God, `God-breathed,' the product of the creative breath of God. In a word, that which is declared by this fundamental passage is simply that the Scriptures are a Divine product, without any indication of how God has operated in producing them. No term could have been chosen, however, which have more emphatically asserted the Divine production of Scripture than that which is here employed. The "breath of God" is in Scripture just the symbol of His almighty power, the bearer of His

2

creative word. *"By the word of Jehovah,* we read in the significant parallel of Psalm 33:6, *"were the heavens made, and all the host of them by the breath of his mouth."* And it is particularly where the operations of God are energetic that this term is employed to designate them — God's breath is the irresistible outflow of His power. When Paul declares, then, that `*Every Scripture,'* or, `*all Scripture'* is the product of the Divine breath, `*is God- breathed,'* he asserts with as much energy as he could employ that Scripture is the product of a specifically Divine operation."

The Bible being Divine, every word is precious:

"As His divine power has given to us all things [pertaining] to life and god- liness through the full knowledge of the [One] having called us through glory and virtue, by which means He has given to us the very great and precious promises, so that through these you might be partakers of [the] divine nature, escaping from the corruption in [the] world by lust" (2 Peter 1:3, 4).

Are not words precious that promise believers in Christ that *"He has given to us the precious promise that we might be partakers of the divine nature"*? Is that not what every believer in Christ aspires to be, to be like God? Surely, no believer could cling to the fleshly thought that they would rather be like themselves than like God.

When one reads through the Scriptures from Genesis to Revelation, it becomes quite evident that you must be *"transformed by the renewing of your mind'* (Romans 12:2) if you are to become *"conformed to the image of the Son of Him"* (that is, *"of God"* -Romans 8:29). For when the Spirit gives spiritual life to a soul, then by His Word He activates it to transform it and conform it to become *"a partaker of [the] divine nature."* (2 Peter 1:4)

B. The use of the Word in regeneration:
"Blessed [be] the God and Father of our Lord Jesus Christ. He according to His great mercy having generated

us again (Strong's #313 - ανα = again; #1080 - γεννησας = generated) to a living hope through [the] resurrection of Jesus Christ from [the] dead" . . . . *"having been generated again, not by corruptible seed, but incorruptible, through the living Word of God . . . "* (1 Peter 1:3, 23)

Warfield continues, demonstrating the powerful meaning of the text of 2 Timothy 3:15: "In the passage in which Paul makes this energetic assertion of the Divine origin of Scripture he is engaged in explaining the greatness of the advantages which Timothy had enjoyed for learning the saving truth of God. He had had good teachers; and from his very infancy he had been, by his knowledge of the Scriptures, made wise unto salvation through faith in Jesus Christ; he had not only had good instructors, but also always 'an open Bible,' as we should say, in his hand. To enhance yet further the great advantage of the possession of these Sacred Scriptures the apostle adds now a sentence throwing their nature strongly up to view. They are of Divine origin, and therefore of the highest value for all holy purposes."

C. God's words comprise a legacy, a testament
"so shall MY Word be, which goes out of My mouth; it shall not return to Me void, but it shall accomplish that which I please, and it shall prosper in what I sent it to do" (Isaiah 55:11)

Here and many other places God identifies the Scriptures as HIS Word. And in this verse He states that what He has purposed, He will most certainly accomplish. This would, of course, include the promises that are embedded throughout God's Word, and certifies that they will be honored to those who are members of His family, *"heirs and co-heirs with Christ"* (Romans 8:17)

Would one who had received the benefits of a will that contained *"great and precious promises"* be content merely to read only a few paragraphs of that will? If some of these precious benefits were buried in small print in a section that at first sight appeared to be unimportant, would it be sensible to simply skip over and ignore that section? Would not any beneficiary read every word of that will? Yes, and he or she would read it over and over to make sure that every benefit that had been conferred would be discovered, and immediately accepted with much thanksgiving!

How much more important is every word of God's will and testament to His elect children! Everything that pertains *"to life and godliness"* (2 Peter 1:3) is implanted (James 1:21) in the Scriptures. Who could be content to have only a little life and a little godliness because it took time and attention to read every word that would convey vibrant spiritual life and godliness? You must read the Testaments through if you are to know all the wonderful things that God has willed to you.

D. Jesus demonstrated that every word of Scripture is God's Word

A reading of the Gospels will reveal that Jesus quoted copiously from the Scriptures, that He regarded every syllable of them as of absolute authority (some 45% of the words of Jesus in the Gospels are quotations of Old Testament scriptures). Not even a jot or a tittle (*"one iota or one point"* (Matthew 5:18; John 10:34). may pass away, for *"the Scripture cannot be broken."* Why? It is because the very formation of each letter was written by the prophets and apostles as the Holy Spirit bore them along. Since all things to come to pass had been decreed as God's Word from eternity: *"for prophecy was not at any time by [the] will of man, but having been borne along by [the] Holy Spirit holy men of God spoke"* (2 Peter 1:21). One being borne has no choice of his own, but must conform entirely to the will of the one who bears him. Christ, being both God and man, of course knew every jot and tittle of the preordained Scriptures. He silenced Satan in the temptation by merely saying "It is written," giving exactly the words written in the Old Testament Scriptures. So it was with the Scripture writers, including the Gospel writers who record what Jesus said. They were so borne along as to write only the words that God the Spirit had ordained to be written as Scripture. Did the Spirit dictate the words to the writers? No! Rather, from birth He nurtured those who would be the writers of the Scriptures so as for them to come to the day, the special character, and development of spiritual nature, that they could and would think the thoughts of God after

5

Him and write the eternal words He had decreed.

Is God able to put thoughts into men's minds? Yes, *"For God gave into their hearts to do His mind, and to act in one mind"* (Revelation 17:17). And this is spoken of unbelieving opposers of God. How much more He can and does put into the minds and hearts of His children the thoughts which will bring them to do His mind.

II. GOD COMMANDS THAT EVERYONE KNOW HIS WORD

"If you continue in My Word, you are truly My disciples. And you will know the truth, and the truth will set you free" (John 8:31, 32)

"Therefore you shall obey the voice of Jehovah your God and do His commandments and His statutes which I command you today" (Deuteronomy 27:10)

The voice of God resounds in our hearts and mind through the reading of His Word. He speaks to us as we read, and as one continues meditation will bring that voice back through memory, and will further implant its meaning into our hearts.
"In meekness receive the implanted Word being able to save your souls. But become doers of [the] Word, and not hearers only, deceiving yourselves" (James 1:21, 22).

Having had the Word implanted in your soul, growth in grace and knowledge of the Lord Jesus Christ (2 Peter 3:18) will make one a doer of the Word. And as verses 23 and 24 states, if one looks into the Word as a hearer only, it will result in forgetfulness, leaving no fruit. But verse 25 informs the reader,

"looking into the perfect law of liberty, and <u>continuing in it</u>, this one not having become a forgetful hearer, but a doer of [the] work, this one will be blessed in his doing." (James 1:25)

There can be no knowing of the truth until the source of the truth is searched. In His high-priestly prayer to God the Father, the Lord Jesus tells where that is to be found, *"Your Word is truth."* (John 17:17). And in John 16:13, the welcome promise is made,*"He* [God the Holy Spirit] *will guide you into all truth."*

To summarize: (a) Through the Word, one knows the truth; (b) the truth will set one free, (c) that freedom will enable one to obey the truth, the commandments, and, (d) the beneficiary of all this grace becomes a doer of the Word, (e) during which practice the Spirit of God guides the doer into all truth; (f) blessing after blessing is bestowed on the reader of the Word.

All of these benefits cannot take place without the implanting of the Word in the heart, and that requires the reading of the Word, or hearing it preached in depth.

III. THE LEGITIMATE DESIRES OF THE HEART CAN BE SOUGHT AND OBTAINED BY OBSERVING THE GOD-GIVEN DIRECTIONS IN THE HOLY SCRIPTURES

Untold and immeasurable blessings are to be found by any diligent reader of God's Word in its entirety. The following twenty-six much sought after desires will illustrate the fullness of the Scriptures, and the assurance that they are set forth as attainable by anyone reading and obeying the truth outlined in them.

A. Everlasting life

1. It is given through regeneration
"Jesus answered, Truly, truly, I say to you, if not one is generated of water and of Spirit, he is not able to enter into the kingdom of God. That having been generated out of the flesh is flesh, and that having been generated of water and of Spirit is spirit. Do not wonder that I said to you, You must be generated from above. The Spirit breathes where

He desires, and you hear his voice, but you do not know from where He comes, and where He goes; so is everyone who has been generated from the Spirit" (John 3:5-8)

Everlasting life is given through regeneration by the Holy Spirit. He uses the Word of God as a means of conveying the fruits from this everlasting life.

2. The instrument used by the Spirit is the Word of God

"It is the Spirit [who] gives life. The flesh does not profit; nothing! The words which I speak to you are spirit and are life" (John 6:63)

The Holy Spirit of God authored the Bible so that those reading it might have life through the Word.

"But these have been written that you may believe that Jesus is the Christ, the Son of God, and that believing you may have life in His name" (John 20:31)

3. This everlasting life is in God's Son

"I am the Way, the Truth, and the Life" (John 14:6)

"And this is the witness, that God gave us everlasting life, and this life is in His Son. The [one] having the Son has life. The [one] not having the Son of God does not have life" (1 John 5:11, 12)

All things came into being through Him, and without Him not even one [thing] came into being (John 1:3).

How much more true is this of everlasting life. Without Him no one can have everlasting life.

4. Authority to become the children of God is given by the Son

"But as many as received Him, to them He gave authority to become children of God, to the ones believing into His name, who were generated, not of bloods, nor of [the] will of [the] lesh, nor of [the] will of man, but of God" (John 1:12, 13)

This He spoke clearly in His high priestly prayer:

"Jesus spoke these things and lifted up His eyes to Heaven, . . . Even as You gave to Him authority over all flesh, so that to all which You gave to Him, He may give to them everlasting life. And this is everlasting life, that they may know You, the only true God, and Jesus Christ, whom You have sent" (John 17:1-3)

5. It is possible to know whether one has everlasting life

"Truly, truly, I say to you, the [one] believing into Me has everlasting life" (John 6:47)
"Truly, truly, I say to you, the [one] hearing My Word, and the [One] having sent Me, has everlasting life, and does not come into judgment, but has passed out of death into life." (John 5:24)

The new creature generated by the Spirit will learn from the Word that everlasting life already exists in his or her soul, that they have passed out of death into life.

6. Sin brings death for all who are not in Christ
"For the wages of sin [is] death, but the free gift of God [is] everlasting life in Christ Jesus our Lord" (Romans 6:13)

All who seek to obtain everlasting life through any other way shall be found guilty of unrepentant sin at the Judgment Seat of Christ:

9

"We all must appear before the Judgment Seat of Christ, so that each one may receive the things [done] through the body, according to what he did, whether good or bad" (2 Corinthians 5:10)

B. Salvation through the faith that is a gift of God, the remission of all your sins, past, present, and future, and the adoption into the Divine family as a child of God

1. Salvation through faith

"For by grace you are saved, through faith, and this not of yourselves; [it is] the gift of God" (Ephesians 2:8)

"Everyone who believes that Jesus is the Christ has been generated of God" (1 John 5:1)

Spiritual life must precede faith, for there can be no exercise of any grace without life:

"The [one] believing into the Son has everlasting life."
There is no believing into the Son until one has spiritual life. One must be generated from above and thus be given this life that is everlasting:

"Truly, truly, I say to you, if one is not generated from above he is not able to see the kingdom of God" (John 3:3).

"It is the Spirit who gives life. The flesh does not profit; nothing! The words that I speak to you are spirit and are life" (John 6:63).

(a) Faith comes through the Word of God

"Faith comes by hearing, hearing by the Word of God" And spiritual life, everlasting life, is necessary before the hearing of the Word of God, and hearing the Word of God precedes *faith*. This

hearing of the Word of God may be internally received by reading the Word of God. But God has ordained the preaching of the word as the normal method of presenting the Word of God: *"And how may they believe [One] of whom they have not heard? And how may they hear without preaching?"* (Romans 10:14)

2. Remission of all sins

"Then let it be known to you, men, brothers, that through this One remission of sins is announced to you" (Acts 13:38)

The remission of sins through Christ is a complete exemption from punishment for sins, and this is for believers only.
"And almost all things are cleansed by blood according to the Law, and without shedding of blood no remission occurs" (Hebrews 9:22)

"the blood of His Son Jesus Christ cleanses us from all sin" (1 John 1:7)

It is important to note that "Jesus Christ cleanses us from **"all sin"** through His blood. This remission includes the full and complete forgiveness for all past sins, all present sins, and all sins yet to be committed by the one who is being cleansed from sins through that precious blood of Christ. This is essential because God's elect children must appear before God without blame or blemish.

The word translated as remission is αφεσις *(aphesis -* Strong's #859). Properly it means "the letting things go, as if they had never been committed" *(Thayer's Lexicon,* p. 88a) . It is more than forgiveness in the sense that forgiveness ordinarily bears; it is more than pardon of a prisoner, it is the washing clean of the believer as if there had never been any sin.

"even from Jesus Christ the faithful witness, the First-born out of the dead, and the Ruler of the kings of the

11

earth. To Him loving us and washing us from our sins by His blood, and made us kings and priests to God, even the Father. To Him [is] the glory and the might forever and ever" (Revelation 1:5)

"I will not at all still remember their sins and their lawless deeds, but where remission of these [is] there [is] no more offering concerning sins." (Hebrews 10:17, 18; Jeremiah 31:33,34)

And this cleansing through the blood of Christ, like everything done by Him, was accomplished once for all at the time of His sacrificial death. All blood-bought believers enjoy the fruits of the comprehensive atonement purchased by Christ on the Cross..

(a) The giving of everlasting life reveals the remission of sins
"to open their eyes,and to turn [them] from darkness to light, and [from] the authority of Satan to God, in order that they [may[receive remission of sins, and an inheritance among those being sanctified by faith in Me" (Acts 26:18)

3. Adoption as children of God

"For you did not receive a spirit of slavery again to fear, but you received a Spirit of adoption by which we cry, Abba! Father! The Spirit Himself witnesses with our spirit that we are children of God. And if children, then also heirs; truly heirs of God and joint heirs of Christ, if indeed we suffer together, that we may also be glorified together" (Rom. 8:15-17)

Life, then faith and repentance, the revealing of remission, then adoption — all these simultaneously, but in that order. All of these are gifts from God to fulfill His eternal purposes (Ephesians 1:11).

"according as He chose us in Him before [the] foundation of [the] world, for us to be holy and without blemish before Him in love, predestinating us to adoption through Jesus Christ to Himself, according to the good pleasure of His will" (Ephesians 1:4, 5).

His beloved, whom He loved with an everlasting love (Jeremiah 31:3), were not intended to be merely pardoned sinners, but were purposed to become children of God, members of His immediate family. And if this were not enough, these same beloved souls were to become *"heirs, truly heirs of God and joint heirs of Christ"* (Romans 8:17).

(a) Not only as members of God's family

"by which means He has given to us the very great and precious promises, so that through these you might be partakers of [the] divine nature, escaping from the corruption in [the] world by lust" (2 Peter 1:4).

It was a very great and precious promise that believers would be children of God. How much more is it that they might be partakers of [the] divine nature!

(b) Redemption of the body

"And not only [so], but also we ourselves having the first-fruit of the Spirit, also we ourselves groan within ourselves eagerly expecting adoption, the redemption of our body;" (Romans 8:23)

A further adoption is spoken of here, this one of the redemption of the body. For although the souls of the redeemed have been blessed with cleansing of all sins, the body does not participate in this purity before God while we are in this world:

"Beloved, now we are the children of God, and it was not yet revealed what we shall be. But we know that if He is revealed, we shall be like Him . . ." (1 John 3:2).

Where else but in the Word of God can one learn of such great blessings?

"But when the fullness of time came, God sent forth His Son, having become out of a woman, having come under the Law, that He might redeem the ones under law, that we might receive the adoption of sons" (Gal. 4:4)

Christ the God-man must be born of a woman, be a man under the Law of God, that He might be the Redeemer of His elect people, that they in this way may receive adoption by the Father.

C. Righteousness through the imputing of Christ's sinless life to you, and the fruits of His sacrificial redemptive death for your sins.

1. No descendant of Adam can be righteous by nature:

The depravity of mankind brought on by Adam as man's federal head makes it impossible for anyone to be righteous (Romans 3:10; 1 Corinthians 15:22)

"For if by the offense of the one death reigned through the one, much more those who are receiving the abundance of grace and the gift of righteousness shall rule in life by the One, Jesus Christ" (Romans 5:17)

"Because by works of law not [one of] all flesh will be justified before Him, for through law [is] full knowledge of sin. But now a righteousness of God has been revealed apart from Law and the Prophets, even the righteousness of God through faith of Jesus Christ to all and upon all the

14

[ones] believing; for there is no difference, for all sinned and come short of the glory of God" (Romans 3:20-23)

This is true because no sinner can obey perfectly the law of God.

2. The righteousness of Another must be imputed:

Because the mind of the natural man is at enmity with God (Romans 8:7), a righteousness of a person able to obey the law perfectly must be provided if God is to reckon His elect people as righteous. Since there were none righteous among men, God purposed to take the responsibility of rescuing the elect, and this required Him in the person of God the Son to join with Christ, by which the God-man would become the source of righteousness for them:

"So then, as through the one offense [it was] toward all men to condemnation, so also one accomplished righteousness toward all men to justification of life. For as through the one man's disobedience the many were constituted sinners, so all through the obedience of the One man shall be constituted righteous . . . . so also grace might rule through righteousness to everlasting life, through Jesus Christ our Lord" (Romans 5:18, 19, 21)

The obedience of Christ perfectly fulfilled the law of God, and He being sinless, it could be imputed to others.

3. Christ's accomplished righteousness could be imputed:
"Even as also David says of the blessedness of the man to whom God reckons righteousness apart from works: Blessed [are those] whose lawlessnesses were remitted, and whose sins were covered. Blessed is the man to whom [the] Lord not at all will charge sin"

The righteousness accomplished by the perfect obedience of Christ Jesus then could be reckoned to *"the vessels of mercy"* (Romans 9:23) who were chosen by God to be His elect people.

4. Someone must pay for sin:
"For the wages of sin is death"

"Because of this [Abraham's faith] it was also reckoned to him for righteousness. But it was not written for him only that it was reckoned to him, but also on account of us, to whom it is about to be reckoned, to the ones believing on the [One] who has raised our Lord Jesus from [the] dead, who was delivered for our offenses and was raised for our justification" (Romans 4:6, 7, 22-25; Psalms 32:1,2)

The righteousness of Christ is His righteousness because He lived the perfect life, obeying and thereby satisfying all the demands of God's law. God has revealed in His *Word* that He accepts the imputation of the righteousness of Christ as sufficient ground on which He can justify the believing sinner. The implementation required that Christ be made under the law:

"But when the fulness of time came, God sent forth His Son, having become of a woman, having become under Law, that He might redeem the ones under law, that we might receive the adoption of sons" (Galatians 4:4)

By His perfect obedience to the law, Christ did not end or abolish the law, but He fulfilled it; He satisfied entirely the demands of the law as to obedience. Having lived this perfect, sinless life, it was made ready to impute His perfect righteousness to all the ones believing into Him (John 6:47)..

Yet the sin debt must be paid. So God's plan of salvation called for God the Son, though subsisting in the form of God, to empty *"Himself, taking the form of a slave, becoming in [the] likeness of men;"* (Philippians 2:7)

And by joining Himself to Christ, and taking the form of a slave, though in truth God-man, *" and being found in fashion as a man, He humbled Himself, becoming obedient until death, even [the] death of the cross"* (Philippians 2:6-8).

5. By His death regeneration, justification by faith, repentance, and remission were purchased:
"Therefore take heed to yourselves and to all the flock, . . . to shepherd the church of God which He purchased through [His] own blood" (Acts 20:28)

God chose to accept the righteousness of Christ as the righteousness of all believers, and this was accomplished by simply reckoning to them the righteousness of Christ instead of the unrighteousness of the fallen men, they being justified through the law of faith.

"But now a righteousness of God has been revealed apart from Law, being witnessed to by the Law and the Prophets, even the righteousness of God through faith of Jesus Christ toward all and upon all those believing" (Romans 3:21, 22).

This righteousness is not infused into the sinner. The sinner does not become righteous in his or her person. Rather the righteousness of Christ is put upon, envelops these sinners, and it is reckoned to them as a gift of God. God then sees the righteousness of Christ when He looks upon the sinner clothed in that perfect righteousness. Perfect obedience having been accomplished, and the sin-debt having been paid by the death of Christ, justification was assured for each one of the persons for whom He died:

"Who will bring [any] charge against God's elect? God is the [One] justifying! Who [is] the [one] condemning. Christ [is] the [One] having died, but also rather also [is He] having been raised, . . . (Romans 8:33, 34)
Only in this way can a sinner be justified in God's sight, and made fit to be an everlasting dweller in a holy Heaven in the presence of the infinitely holy Trinity.

Where else but in God's revelation in His Scriptures can be found the way that a totally depraved sinner may become just before God. One must read the Bible through and through to learn the extent of this marvelous provision, to absorb the knowledge of it, and to savor it more and more until that Day when those reckoned righteous will stand at the right hand of God.

"Go away from Me, cursed ones, into the everlasting fire having been prepared for the Devil and his angels" (Matthew 25:41).

Also revealed in the Scriptures is the fact that all not believing into Jesus will be on the left hand of God, to whom it will be said, *"Go away from Me . . . into the everlasting fire."*

D. Blessedness (The highest form of happiness)

"No, rather, blessed [are] those hearing the Word of God, and keeping it" (Luke 11:28)

"Blessed [is] the [one] reading, and those hearing, the words of this prophecy, and keeping the things having been written; . . ." (Revelation 1:3)

"Blessed [is the one] You choose and cause to come near You; (Psalm 65:4)

The most famous verses displaying the depth and the breadth of God's blessings are Matthew 5:3 through 5:12. The natural mind, being at enmity with God (Romans 8:7), despises the blessings set forth there in The Beatitudes. Where is the comfort for the unbeliever in being poor in spirit, mourning, meek, righteous, pure, peacemakers, being persecuted ones, and needing mercy? But the spiritual mind discerns all things (1 Corinthians 2:15), especially *"the things which God has prepared for those that love Him"* (Isaiah 64:4).

"Blessed are the poor in spirit" - that is, *the poor in spirit,* (not in worldly goods), for they have the *"unsearchable riches of Christ"* (Ephesians 3:8)

18

"Blessed [are] they who mourn, for they shall be comforted" - (or ***encouraged***,) as the word may be translated.

A. T. Robertson (*Robertson's Word Pictures*) calls this "another paradox" (p. 40). But there are NO paradoxes in the Scriptures, only a charley-horse between the ears of those who say so (this is Dr. Gordon H. Clark's famous explanation).

"Blessed [are] the meek, for they shall inherit the earth,"
a quotation from Psalm 37:11

From a spiritual standpoint, [*meek* is] the most misunderstood word in the English language. English dictionaries are composed by worldly men, and to them the word meekness is despicable. Homer, the unbelieving German critics, and Westcott and Hort thought of meekness as mildness, gentility. Equally wide of the mark are modern version translators (the NIV translates #6035 meek only once, elsewhere they juggle humble, afflicted, poor, needy and gentle, not able to make up their minds).

What then is the meaning of *meek*? Moses was meek above all men (Numbers 12:3); David uses the word and its cognates a dozen times; and the Lord Jesus was meek (Matthew 11:29; 21:5). Stoic resignation is not meekness. Trapp defines it as "to bear and to forbear." The concept of meekness needs a large exposition because it is a unique trait as evidenced by its distinguishing use here. Note these descriptive words:

"The meek is an appellation which describes the temper of mind under suffering. The persons here spoken of here are viewed, not as enjoying unbroken prosperity, but as exposed to affliction in a variety of forms; and when exposed, they are not fretful, discontented, resentful, but meek, quiet, resigned, cheerful, sufferers. Patience and meekness are nearly allied [in that] *patience* is expressive of the sufferer's temper in reference to his sufferings; *meekness* is expressive of his temper in reference to those who are the authors or occasions of his sufferings. Our afflictions may be viewed as coming from God, or as coming from our fellow men; and meekness is the name of that disposition which we should cherish, and which every Christian, so far as he is under the influence of Christian principle, does cherish, both in reference to God and man viewed as the cause or the occasion of suffering to us.

"Like all other holy tempers described in this passage, meekness originates in a right view of the Divine character, and of our own. An enlightened conviction of the infinite greatness and excellence, the sovereignty, . . . the man who believes that God has a right to do with him, as His creature, whatever He pleases; that in the exercise of that right He is uniformly guided by righteousness, wisdom, benignity, and mercy . . . . sees his insignificance as a crea-ture, and his demerit as a sinner, [will have] as the language of his heart, "Here am I, let Him do to me as seems good to Him" (John Brown, *Discourses and Sayings of Our Lord*, p. 69). He cites many references, among them 2 Corinthians 5:19; Romans 8:28, 32; 9:21; Deuteronomy 8:5; 2 Samuel 15;26; Acts 21:14; Lamentations 3:22,26,28,31,32,33,39; Micah 6:9; 7:9; Hebrews 12:7,8. To these add, Psalm 39:9, 1 Peter 3:4.

Was Moses gentle? Ask Korah. Was the Lord Jesus mild? Ask the scribes and Pharisees.

"Blessed [are] they who hunger and thirst after righteous-ness, for they shall be filled" = that is, *shall be fully satis-fied. See Satisfaction below.*

"Blessed are the merciful, they shall obtain mercy,"

These are those "that from a compassionate heart (melting with sense of God's everlasting mercy to itself, and yearning over the miseries of others) extend and exercise spiritual and corporal mercy" (*Trapp's Commentary on the New Testament*, p. 47 - here-after, (TCNT).

"Blessed [are] the pure in heart, for they shall see God"

"holiness, without which no one will see the Lord"
(Hebrews 12:14)

These are "those who, like the good angels, are always seeing God," (TCNT, p. 49) [who] *"with unveiled face behelding the glory of [the] Lord in a mirror, are being changed [into] the same image from glory to glory, as from [the] Lord Spirit"* (2 Corinthians 3:18 - See also Psalms 15:2; 24:4; 73:1;).

"Blessed are the peacemakers, for they shall be called sons of God!"

"Blessed [are] those being persecuted for righteousness' sake."

Being persecuted is not a blessed thing. But the one being persecuted for the sake of righteousness will find his or her own righteousness abiding, and will reap the fruits of righteousness (2 Corinthians 9:9, 10) — *persecute you = pursue you in order to harass, trouble and molest you* is the meaning of the word (Strong's #1377); "eagerly pursue and follow you hot-foot, as the hunter does the prey" (TCNT, p. 51). See 1 Peter 4:14; John 15:20, where Jesus says, *"If they have persecuted Me, also they will persecute you."*

What then? *"Rejoice and leap for joy, for your reward [is] in Heaven"*.

E. Holiness, sanctification, perfection

1. Holiness is an attribute of God

Holiness is an attribute of God. It is a glorious perfection belonging to the nature of God, and that is why He is so often called The Holy One. This attribute belongs to God the Father, God the Son, and God the Holy Spirit, because they are one God, sharing the same essence (Hebrews 1:3). Only God can be perfectly holy. *"Holy, holy, holy is Jehovah of hosts, the whole earth [is] full [of] His glory"* (Isaiah 6:3). This cannot be said of even the most sanctified of saints.

21

In what way is God holy? Basically, the word carries the meaning of separation. God is separate from mankind in every respect. He is above and beyond in His being, in His eternity, and so with all His attributes. One thing especially marks His holy actions. In all His thoughts, His purposes, His decrees which precede His actions, He needs only to please Himself.

2. The saints of God may pursue holiness

"but according to the Holy One who has called you, you also become holy in all conduct; because it has been written, Be holy because I am holy" (1 Peter 1:15, 16; Leviticus 19:2)

In the process of sanctification which proceeds throughout the life of believers, degrees of holiness may be attained:

"Eagerly pursue peace with all, and holiness, without which no one will see the Lord" (Hebrews 12:14)

"I call upon you through the compassions of God to present your bodies a living sacrifice, holy, well-pleasing to God [which is] your reasonable service" (Romans 12:1)

"Then having these promises, beloved, let us purify ourselves from all defilement of flesh and of spirit, perfecting holiness in [the] fear of God" (2 Corinthians 7:1)

In the highest degree of holiness which is achievable by the saints of God, their thoughts must follow God's thoughts (as expressed in His Word, therefore with His purposes. Their actions must be in accordance with His Word, as the highest revelation of His thinking toward mankind). Their purposes must be aligned if the achievable degree of holiness is to be realized. To please Him must become the consuming desire of the saint's heart. It is for this reason that it is written, *"Be holy because I am holy."*

3. Sanctification unto holiness is purchased by Christ

"Sanctify them in Your truth. Your Word is truth" (John 17:17)

Holiness in any degree is a gift of God. Only God can make one holy. And through the life and death of Christ He does constitute them to be holy. But there is a sense in which believers in this life may pursue holiness. This is a gradual process, and it is only possible through Jesus Christ, who *"was made to us . . . sanctification,"* and who prays for all those who were given to Him (John 17:9) that God would sanctify them in His truth (John 17:17). And the sanctification in that same prayer indicates that this only can be done through God's Word. Holiness then is the state of being in conformity with God's will, and sanctification is the deed or process by which that state of holiness is worked.

But the working is of God:
"So as, my beloved, even as you always obeyed, not as in my presence only, but now much rather in my absence, cultivate your salvation with fear and trembling. For God is the [One] working in you both to will and to work for the sake of [His] good pleasure" (Philippians 3:12, 13).

To translate #2716 as "work out your own salvation" sets up a contradiction between Ephesians 2:8-10 where God says that faith (and so salvation) is a gift of God. It is not of works, that it might be of faith. The right translation of Strong's #2716 is "Cultivate" or, "Develop," it is a compound word that means to work thoroughly, or throughout, that which is yours. It is in the same sense that one works the land that he owns. God has given salvation to you, now you are to cultivate this so-great salvation that has been freely given.

4. This is the sanctification, the mark, the prize, that Paul stretched forward to lay hold of.
Throughout the epistles you see what occurs in this process of sanctification:

"Think this among you, which [mind was] in Christ Jesus;" (Philippians 2:5*); "but speaking truth in love, we may grow up into Him in all things who is the Head, the Christ"* (Ephesians 4:15*); "purify ourselves from all defilement. . . perfecting holiness in the fear of God"* (2 Corinthians 7:1*); "so also we might walk in newness of life"* (Romans 6:4); *"present yourselves to God as [one] living from [the] dead, and your members instruments of righteousness to God"* (Romans 6:13*); "yield your members [as] slaves to righteousness unto sanctification. . . . But now being set free from sin, but having been enslaved to God, you have your fruit unto sanctification and the end everlasting life"* (Romans 6:19, 22).

Sanctification is God's work, beginning with regeneration and the implanting of life everlasting. Then God chooses to complete the sanctification within the person, actively participated in by the saints, under the tutelage and inworking of the Holy Spirit throughout their life. Those who cultivate their salvation will find that **"both He sanctifying, and the [ones] being sanctified [are] all of one, . . . "** (Hebrews 2:11). Then will be an abundant harvest.

F. Purity

1. Purifying is God's work

"by how much more the blood of Christ who through [the] eternal Spirit offered Himself without blemish to God will purify your conscience from dead works so as to serve [the] living God" (Hebrews 9:14)

Throughout the Scriptures it is learned that purity is an essential quality in the nature of God. This is displayed in His freedom from whatever is impure or bespotting, both in His essence and actions.

2. The God-man is the One who made purification of our sins

"who being the shining splendor of [His] glory, and the express image of His essence; and upholding all things by the word of His power, having made purification of our sins through Himself, [He] sat down on the right hand of the Majesty on high" (Hebrews 1:3; Psalm 110:1)

He was of the same essence with the Father and the Spirit, having the same power, yet the wondrous plan of salvation was planned so that He could and did make purification of the sins of the saints.

3. This purification is through faith

"And He distinguished nothing between both us and them, having purified their hearts by faith" (Acts 15:9)

The heart-knowing God made no distinction between the nations and the Jews, purifying the hearts of both of them by faith.

4. It is characteristic of the saints to work to purify themselves

"And everyone having this hope on him purifies himself even as that [One] is pure" (1 John 3:3)

Purity in His children also is a work of God, yet there is a sense in which the saint *"purifies himself,"* and this also is done internally in the life through sanctification. The thought also occurs in 1 Peter 1:22, *"having purified your souls in the obedience of the truth through the Spirit."*

It should be recognized that the knowledge of the possibility of this gradual attainment of purity can only be found in the pure Word of God (Psalm 12:6; 119:140)

G. Wisdom

1. Wisdom begins with God

"the fear of Jehovah [is] the beginning of wisdom, and the knowledge of the Holy Ones [is] understanding" (Proverbs

9:10)

"For Jehovah gives wisdom; out of His mouth [are] knowledge
and understanding. He lays up sound wisdom for the
upright, . .." (Proverbs 2:6)

Wisdom is an attribute of God; He is omniscient. He knows everything about everything and about everybody. All wisdom, all knowledge for that matter, originates with God. And wisdom originates in man with the fear and reverence due to God.

2. God has chosen to impart His wisdom through His Word

"The law of Jehovah [is] perfect, converting the soul. The
testimony of Jehovah [is] sure, making the simple wise"
(Psalm 19:7)

"Behold, You desire truth in the inward parts, and in the
hidden [parts] You teach me wisdom" (Psalm 51:6)

God gives wisdom, and He chooses to do it through His written instructions which are found nowhere else but in the Holy Scriptures. God's Word is truth (John 17:17), and it is through the living, powerfully working Word of God that the new creature is taught the fear of God. And it also is the means of attaining knowledge and understanding. Only in the Scriptures is it learned that *"if anyone thinks to know anything he still has known nothing as he ought to know"* (1 Corinthians 8:2). This fact is reinforced in the life of the apostle Paul, *"I know nothing in myself, "* (1 Corinthians 4:4); and, *"Not that we are sufficient of ourselves to reason out anything as out of ourselves, but our sufficiency is of God"* (2 Corinthians 3:5).

3. Fallen man is not wise, but foolish
"Do not be wise in your own eyes; fear Jehovah and depart
from evil" (Proverbs 3:7; Romans 12:16)

"Professing [themselves] to be wise, they became foolish"
(Romans 1:22)

Since Adam sinned, all his descendants have relied upon their own foolish substitutes for true wisdom. But, *"it has been written, I will destroy the wisdom of the wise, and I will set aside the understanding of the understanding ones"* (1 Corinthians 1:19).

The comparison of the wisdom of men with the wisdom of God is fully covered in 1 Corinthians 1:20 and 2:12, 13. These verses illustrate what God has said about the wisdom of this world:

"Where [is the] wise? Where [the] scribe? Where [is] the lawyer of this world? Did God not make the wisdom of the world foolish? (1:20). *"But we have not received the spirit of the world, but the Spirit from God, so that we might know the things that are freely given to us by God, which things we also speak, not in words taught in human wisdom, but in [words] taught of the Holy Spirit, comparing spiritual things with spiritual"* (2:12, 13)

4. As in all things, wisdom is through Christ

" But to the "called out ones . . . Christ [is] the power of God and the wisdom of God." (1 Corinthians 1:24)

"Of Christ, in whom are hidden all the treasures of wisdom and of knowledge" (Colossians 2:3)

As God He knew all, and as Man He personified the wisdom of God.

H. Reproof, correction, and instruction so that you may be complete, fully furnished for every good work

> *"Every Scripture [is] God-breathed and profitable for doctrine, for reproof, for correction, for instruction in righteousness, so that the man of God may be complete, having been furnished for every good work"* (2 Timothy 3:16, 17)

1. Doctrine

Doctrine is the body of truth that the Heaven-bound saints believe. Secular doctrine consists in self-generated theory. Spiritual doctrine is not merely theory, but it is the system of belief firmly and fully taught in the Scriptures. This belief of all the doctrines written in God's Word is **not** optional.

2. Reproof

> *"Every word of God [is] tested. He [is] a shield to those who seek refuge in Him. Do not add to His words, that He not reprove you, and you be found a liar"* (Proverbs 30:5, 6)

It is usual with God to do His reproving through His written Word, or through one preaching from the Scriptures.

> *"You shall not hate your brother in your heart. You shall certainly reprove your neighbor and not allow sin on him"* (Leviticus 19:17)

> *"Let the righteous strike me; [it is] a mercy; and he rebuking me, [it is] oil of the head, let not my head refuse [it];"* (Psalm 141:5)

> *"The ear that hears the reproof of life shall remain among the wise. He who ignores correction despises his own soul, but he who hears reproof gets understanding"* (Proverbs 15:31, 32)

Yet it is also a duty and a favor for all believers to reprove one another in loving-kindness, remembering that the Word of God is the source of godly reproof, and that such reproof should be according to God's Word.

3. Correction

"My son, do not despise the chastening of [the] Lord, nor faint [while] being corrected by Him. For whom [the] Lord loves, He disciplines, and whips every son whom He receives" (Hebrews 12:5, 6; Proverbs 3:11, 12).

Blessed [is] the man You chasten, O Jehovah; You teach him out of Your law, to give him rest from troubled days, . . ." (Psalm 95:12)

No one is so sanctified or purified before God that no discipline or correction is needed at times. Besides, apart from possible courses of sin, there are times in the life of everyone when a change of direction may be in God's plans. In either case, the Scriptures are so constructed as to teach the reader the ways of God, and thus to instruct him or her either how to avoid being disciplined, or how to bear up under it. Also, the Word of God conditions the reader, sensitizes a person, so that when God makes a correction there is a readiness to accept the change gladly.

4. In the last Day, it will be Christ who judges those who despised His reproof

"The Lord will judge His people" (Hebrews 10:30; Psalm 7:8),

"The [one] who rejects Me and does not receive My words has that judging him, the Word which I spoke, that will judge him in the last Day" (John 12:48)

It will be God the Son who judges on Judgment Day (2 Corinthians 5:10). And all persons will be judged by the Word of

God. Is it not better that all persons study the Scriptures so that they nay learn to judge themselves by the Scriptures? For that is why God has written them, that readers may learn.

I. Satisfaction

"So I will bless You while I live; I will lift up my hands in Your name. My soul shall be satisfied, as [with] marrow and fatness, and my mouth shall praise [You] with joyful lips" (Psalm 63:4, 5)

"Let them thank Jehovah [for] His mercy, and His wonders to the sons of man. He satisfies the thirsty soul, and He fills the hungry soul [with] good" (Psalm 107:9)

"he who is trusting in Jehovah shall be abundantly satisfied" (Proverbs 28:25)

"My people shall be satisfied with My goodness, says Jehovah" (Jeremiah 31:14)

1. Satisfaction is in and by Christ

The ultimate satisfaction is provided only by the life, death, resurrection and intercession of Christ Jesus. (a) He provides atonement for sin; (b) He has settled the sin debt for all believers; (c) He has made complete reparation for the injury and insult that believing sinners have foisted upon God; (d) He has provided complete contentment, pleasure, gratification to those who believe and act upon His Word; (e) He intercedes both for the successes and failures of His sheep; (f) He provides entry into Heaven where perfect satisfaction will rest in the souls of every one of His lambs.

2. Satisfaction in this life is through Christ

Through Christ there is satisfaction provided for every condition of the regenerated sinner: (a) for the burdened (Matthew 11:28); (b) for the hungry and thirsty (Psalm 107:9); (c) for the broken-hearted (Luke 4:18; Isaiah 61:1; Psalm 51:17); (d) riches for the poor; (e) tears (Isaiah 25:8); (d) for all other needs and yearnings (Proverbs 28:25; Philippians 4:19). See **blessedness J. Contentment**

1. Contentment is attainable only through Christ

"I have strength for all things [through] Christ, the [One] strengthening me. . . . And my God will fill your every need according to the riches in glory in Christ Jesus" (Philippians 4:13, 19)

The riches in glory purchased for the lambs of Christ will fill every need of the regenerate heart. To have contentment all one needs to do is to follow the instructions He gives in His Word. Contentment, like everything else that the godly person has been given, has been bought and paid for by Christ Jesus:
Are you a child of God? Bought and paid for.
Are you an heir, even co-heir with Christ? Bought and paid for by Him.
Are you a partaker of the divine nature? It is a gift from Christ, bought and paid for by His life and sacrificial death.
Having reached such heights, far beyond all your dreams, do you still harbor some discontent within you? Get rid of whatever is causing it. Take up the promises throughout the Scriptures. Write beside each one, "Tried and proven." Find them and take your spiritual temperature. Take counsel with the Great Physician, confess your ailments, and get His prescription for contentment. And, mind you, do not stop taking what He prescribes until you have finished excising every lingering fever of discontent.

2. To obtain full contentment, the Christian must focus on Christ

In one of the greatest Christian classics of all time, *The Rare Jewel of Christian Contentment*, the puritan Jeremiah Burroughs teaches that contentment comes by way of subtraction, rather than by addition. He cites Psalm 73:23, 25:

31

"Yet I [was] continually with You. You have taken hold of my right hand. . . . Whom have I in Heaven? And I have no desire on earth besides You"

The secret of contentment, says Burroughs, is to subtract from your desires again and again until you only have this one great desire, to be conformed to the image of Christ Jesus, and so to please Him in everything, and at all times.

There is a mystery in this, in that the saints are the most satisfied persons on earth, and at the same time they are the most dissatisfied on earth. They are satisfied with godliness, find it of great gain. Yet they will never be fully satisfied with anything on earth; in fact they will not be completely satisfied until they are taken away from earth into the presence of their adored Savior.

The carnal person, on the contrary, envisions the addition of this, and then that, and then something more, he professes that he will be satisfied at each stage. But there is no contentment outside of Christ, for all unbelievers are counted as wicked persons in rebellion against their Maker, who states:

"The wicked are like the driven sea, which cannot be quiet, and its waves cast up mire and dirt. There is no peace to the wicked, says my God" (Isaiah 57:20, 21)

And where else can this contentment be found, except in the Holy Scriptures of God?

K. Freedom

1. Christ has made a gift of freedom to those who believe into Him

"Then stand firm in the freedom with which Christ made us free, and do not be held again with a yoke of slavery" (Galatians 5:1)

There are many kinds of imprisonment, or slavery, for an unregenerated sinner: darkness, sin, futility, hopelessness, Satan, *"lusts of the flesh, lusts of the eye, and the pride of life"* (Romans 7:24, 1 John 2:15), death, suffering, etc. Christ alone can free sinners from every kind of slavery

2. The purchase of freedom is ministered through the Spirit

"And the Lord is the Spirit, and where the Spirit of [the] Lord [is] there [is] freedom" (2 Corinthians 3:17)

"If you continue in My Word you are truly My disciples, and you will know the truth, and the truth will set you free" (John 8:31, 32)

The Spirit of God puts forth His lifegiving power to create life, generating a newborn child of God. Then the truth is revealed, and the truth sets him or her free from all those forms of bondage.

"But also if our gospel be hidden, it has been hidden in those being lost, in whom the god of this age has blinded the thoughts of the unbelieving, so that the brightness of the glory of Christ (who is the image of God), should not dawn on them" (2 Corinthians 4:3, 4)

The truth of the gospel had been hidden because Satan had blinded the eyes of those not believing into Christ. When the Spirit gives new life, spiritual life, then it is that *"the brightness of the glory of Christ"* dawns on the new creature in Christ Jesus.

[Now] having been born again, not by corruptible seed, but incorruptible, through the living Word of God, and remaining forever . . . . as newborn babes desire the pure soul-nourishing milk, that you may grow by it; if indeed you tasted that the Lord is good" (1 Peter 1:23; 2:2. 3; Psalm 34:8)

The *"soul-nourishing milk"* mentioned there is the *"Word of [the] Lord [that] remains forever"* (1 Peter 1:25). The soul delivered from the bondage of sin yearns to *"grow in grace and in the knowledge of the Lord Jesus Christ"* (2 Peter 3:18). To enjoy the maximum freedom, one must continue to read, meditate upon, and have confidence in the instructions given in the Scriptures. If the truth is expected to set us free day by day, it must be remembered that Jesus declared in His high priestly prayer, *"My Word is truth."* Then surely that is where one must go to find the truth if one is to be set free from the shackles of sin and Satan.

L. Peace

1. It is God who makes peace

"I [am] Jehovah, and there is none else. Forming light, and creating darkness, <u>making peace</u>, and creating evil" (Isaiah 45:6, 7).

Who could give peace other than the God of peace? Without God there is no peace:

2. This peace is given solely through Jesus Christ, the Mediator between God and men

"Be anxious about nothing, but in everything by prayer and petition with thanksgivings let your requests be made known to God. And the peace which surpasses all understanding will keep your hearts and your minds in Christ Jesus" (Philippians 4:6, 7)

"Then having been justified by faith, we have peace with God through our Lord Jesus Christ" (Romans 5:1)

3. There is no peace to the despisers of salvation available through Christ:
"But the wicked are like the driven sea, which cannot be quiet, and its waves cast up mire and dirt. Thee is no peace to the wicked, says my God" (Isaiah 57:21).

34

Anyone whose peace is disturbed needs to apply to the Maker of peace, who is God, and this only through His elect Savior, Jesus Christ: His recipe for peace He has written out clearly:

"Come unto Me all those laboring and being burdened, and I will give you rest. Take My yoke upon you and learn from Me" (Matthew 11:28, 29)

4. The peace that passes understanding is also a gift of Christ

"And the peace of God, which surpasses all understanding, will keep your hearts and your minds in Christ Jesus" (Philippians 4:7)

"I have spoken these things to you that you may have peace in Me. You have distress in the world, but be encouraged, I have overcome the world" (John 16:33)
"I leave peace to you; My peace I give to you. Not as the world gives I give to you. Let not your heart be agitated, nor let it be fearful" (John 14:17)

This peace, too, like all the precious gifts of God to His children, is among the things that Christ Jesus has purchased for His sheep:

5. It is God's method to apply the purchases of Christ through the Spirit

From the Word, we find that it is God the Spirit who applies this peace that passes all understanding: *"The fruit of the Spirit is love, joy, peace . . . ."* (Galatians 5:22).

6. Being a Christian is not a passive experience
"And let the peace of God rule in your hearts, to which you were called in one body, and be thankful. Let the Word of Christ dwell in you richly, in all wisdom, teaching and exhorting yourselves in Psalms and hymns and

spiritual songs, singing with grace in your hearts to the Lord" (Colossians 3:15, 16).

It is plain that those who have believed into Christ (John 6:47) are directed to actively pursue the wisdom of the Word, and to exhort themselves by all means provided, including singing and psalming (Incidentally, the "hymns" and "spiritual songs" spoken of in verse sixteen also are portions of the Holy Scriptures. They do not refer to the hymns that are written by men, however sweetly they reflect the teachings of the Scriptures.)

The Word of God will not dwell in one richly unless there is a thorough search of the Scriptures for the clues that set the pattern for peace in the heart. And *"as iron sharpens iron, so a man sharpens his friend's face"* (Proverbs 27:17). Teaching, exhorting, and singing the praises of our blessed Lord Jesus Christ will bring peace to the soul of the friends who share their joy in Christ with you.

M. Joy

1. God is the ultimate provider of joy

"I will greatly rejoice in Jehovah. My soul shall be joyful in my God. For He clothed me [with] garments of salvation. He put on me the robe of righteousness, . . . " (Isaiah 61:10)

How could anyone not be joyful in God when He has so richly clothed him or her in the garments of salvation?

2. Every blessing of the soul is through Christ
"whom having not seen you love, in whom not yet seeing, but believing, you exult with unspeakable joy, and having been glorified obtaining the end of your faith, [the] salvation of [your] souls" (1 Peter 1:8, 9).

Unspeakable joy is only to be had through believing into Christ. The joy of a saint in this life may be full and continuous, but the *"unspeakable joy"* will be attained when a saint has been glorified in Heaven. Since there are no time frames in God's thinking, in His mind all things were fully accomplished with His decrees:

"For whom He foreknew, He also predestinated [to be] conformed to the image of His Son, for Him to be [the] First-born among many brothers; and whom He predestinated, these He also called, and whom He called, these He also justified; and whom He justified, these He also glorified" (Romans 8:29,30)

Once in glory, basking in the brightness of the glory of our Savior God, unspeakable joy will be continuous.

3. Again this blessing is ministered through the Spirit of God

"but the fruit of the Spirit is love, joy, peace, long-suffering, kindness, goodness, faith, meekness, self-control. Against such things there is not a law" (Galatians 5:22,23).

The direct source of that joy is God the Spirit, who wondrously works so that the fruit of joy appears in the lives of God's elect sons and daughters

4. God the Spirit authored the Scriptures for our fullness of joy

"we write these things to you that your joy may be full" (1 John 1:4)

And though the words of men cannot describe the uttermost joy, which is reserved for heavenly experience, it is written that full joy may be had through God's Word:

The message is plain: read the Scriptures, for there is abundant joy tucked away here and there in various books of the Bible.

37

This is so in order that one may know joy to its fullest extent possible on earth.

N. Love

1. God's love to us.

> *"In this is love, not that we loved God, but that He loved us, and sent His Son [to be] a propitiation relating to our sins. Beloved, if God so loved us, we also ought to love one another. . . . We love Him because He first loved us. . . . "God is love, and the one abiding in love abides in God, and God in him"* (1 John 4 17, 19, 16).

Time is a creature of this world only. In eternity past God chose to create mankind, and He chose to set His love on certain persons, "the elect;" whom He terms His *"vessels of mercy"* (Romans 9:23). He gives a distinct example (in the case of Jacob and Esau, Romans 9:13) that it might be made clear that it was *"that the purpose of God according to election might stand, not of works, but of the [One] calling"* (Romans 9:11). That is why it could be written that *"God first loved us," "the elect of God"* (1 John 4:19; Colossians 3:12; Titus 1:1). The *"beloved of the Lord"* are told, *"God chose you from the beginning to salvation in sanctification of [the] Spirit and belief of the truth"* (2 Thessalonians 2:13).

2. Christ's love is to us, His beloved lambs.

> *"that through faith Christ may dwell in your hearts, having been rooted and having been founded in love, that you may be given strength to grasp with all the saints what [is] the breadth and length and depth and height and to know the surpassing knowledge and love of Christ, that you may be filled to all the fullness of God"* (Ephesians 3:17-20)

What surpassing love it had to be for Christ to leave the serenity of the Godhood, *"who subsisting in the form of God thought it not robbery to be equal with God, but emptied Himself, taking the form of a servant, having become in [the] likeness of men, and being found in fashion as a man, He humbled Himself, having become obedient until death, even [the] death of the cross"* (Philippians 2:6-8)!

3. Our love to Him

"If you love Me, keep My commandments . . . The [one] having My commandments and keeping them, that one is the [one] loving Me, and the [one] loving Me will be loved by My Father, and I will love him and will reveal Myself to him" (John 14:15, 21)

Although The Ten Commandments are a compendium of the commandments of God, the whole of His commandments are in the Scriptures as a complete revelation of God's will for mankind. Because of this, the entire Bible must be read, known, and taken into account when one considers whether God's commandments are being kept. Such examination of self is only possible if one believes into Christ:

"Everyone who believes has been born of God;"

"and this is the witness that God gave us everlasting life, and this life is in His Son. The [one] having the Son has life; the one not having the Son does not have life" (1 John 5:1, 11, 12).

Love for Christ is not possible without spiritual life. Having such love implanted in us as a fruit of the Spirit of God, then we are instructed, *"Little children, let us not love in word, or in tongue, but in deed and in truth"* (1 John 3:18). How is that? Read the thirteenth chapter of Corinthians to discover how love acts, among which are these words:

Love (or, Charity) *"quietly covers all things, believes all things, hopes all things, endures all things. Love never fails"*

"And now faith, hope, and love, these three things remain, but the greatest of these [is] love" (1 Corinthians 13:7, 8, 13).

Once we join Christ in Heaven, only love will be left. For in His presence, there is no longer need for faith or hope, *"for what anyone sees, why does he also hope?"* (Romans 8:24).

O. Hope

1. God gives hope to sinners through the Lord Jesus Christ

"Blessed [be] the God and Father of our Lord Jesus Christ, He according to His great mercy having regenerated us to a living hope through [the] resurrection of Jesus Christ from [the] dead" (1 Peter 1:3).

There would be no hope if God in His mercy had not provided *"a living hope"* that could only be achieved through *"[the] resurrection of Jesus Christ from [the] dead"*

2. Hope is through Christ

"at that time you were without Christ, alienated from the commonwealth of Israel and strangers of the covenants of promise, having no hope and without God in the world" (Ephesians 2:12)

There is no hope worthy of the name except that *"living hope"* which is rooted and grounded in Christ Jesus.

3. Hope for sinners is a revelation of God

"hearing of your faith in Christ Jesus, and the love toward all the saints, because of the hope being laid up for you in Heaven, which you heard before in the Word of the truth of the gospel" (Colossians 1:4, 5)

"For what things were written were written for our instruction, that through patience and encouragement of the Scriptures we might have hope" (Romans 15:5)

The only hope that a sinner may have is revealed through the Word of God. Therefore, it is incumbent upon every living soul to look to the Book where a living hope is promised:

4. Those forgetting God may as well forget about hope.

"The paths of all those forgetting God, and the hope of the ungodly shall perish, whose hope is cut off, and his trust as a spider's house" (Job 8:13, 14)

There is a clear distinction between the ungodly and the believer throughout the Scriptures:

"Through pride of his face, the wicked will not see; there is no God in all of his schemes" (Psalm 10:4)

5. Those enjoying a living hope should witness where it can be found:

"But sanctify the Lord God in your hearts, and always [be] ready to [give] an answer to everyone asking you a reason concerning the hope in you . . ." (1 Peter 3:15)

We must read the Scriptures through and through that we might have hope. For it is chronicled in the Word of God that we may learn to know how to answer those who appear to us to be in need of "a living hope:"

P. Mercy

1. Mercy is an attribute of God.

Mercy is an attribute of God which He may distribute to any creature. Mercy is a kindness, forbearing to visit punishment on offenders. Every breath breathed into the lungs is a mercy, for *"all sinned and come short of the glory of God,"* there being *"none righteous, not one! There is none that understands, there is not one that seeks after God!"* (Romans 3:23, 10, 11). All by nature are *"the children of wrath," "even being dead in sins," "worthy of death"* (Ephesians 2:3, 5; Romans 1:22). In view of this state of the natural man, it is a mercy for God to sustain him in the midst of all his offenses against God. Therefore it is beyond reason for anyone to presume upon God's mercy.

> *"For He said to Moses, I will have mercy on whomever I will have mercy, and I will pity whomever I will pity. So then, [it is] not of the [one] willing, nor of the [one] running, but of the [One] showing mercy, of God"* (Romans 9:15, 16; Exodus 33:19).

God claims the right to distribute His mercy as He desires.

2. God's mercy differs from His grace

> *"as many as had been appointed to eternal life believed"* (Acts 13:48).

Grace is an attribute of God. It is the undeserved favor of God which He bestows upon His elect people from eternity, and displays to them at the time they are regenerated by God the Holy Spirit

3. God's richness in grace and mercy only is displayed in Christ
> *"For the Law was given through Moses, [but] grace and truth came through Jesus Christ"* (John 1:17).

42

"But God, being rich in mercy, because of His great love [with] which He loved us, even we being dead in sins, [He] made us alive together with Christ (by grace you are saved), and raised [us] up together, and seated us together in the heavenlies in Christ Jesus, that He might show us in the coming ages the exceeding great riches of His grace in kindness [mercy] toward us in Christ Jesus" (Ephesians 2:4-7)

Grace, mercy, love, kindness and truth meet together in Christ Jesus (Psalm 85:10). It is through Him that fearers of God receive these great blessings:

4. The Spirit of God regenerates, then pours out these riches which were purchased by Christ

"But when the kindness and love of God our Savior toward man appeared, not by works in righteousness which we had done, but according to His mercy He saved us through [the] washing of regeneration and renewal of the Holy Spirit, whom He poured out on us richly through Jesus Christ our Savior" (Titus 3:4-6)

Only in the words breathed out by the Author of the Scriptures, God the Spirit, is it revealed that we *"being without strength, in due time Christ died for ungodly ones;" "we yet being sinners, Christ died for us;" "being enemies we were reconciled to God through the death of His Son, much more being reconciled we shall be saved by His life"* (Romans 5:6, 8, 10).

Everyone should read all the Scriptures because they are written of Him whose *"mercy endures forever"* (Psalm 136)

R. Self-control

1. Self-control depends on the inworking power of God the Spirit

"but the fruit of the Spirit is love, joy, peace . . . self-control" (Galatians 5:22, 23)

"When wisdom enters into your heart, and knowledge is pleasing to your soul, discretion shall keep you, understanding shall watch over you" (Proverbs 2:10, 11)

By nature people conceive that they are in control of their lives. That is why it is written many times in the Scriptures, *"Be not wise in your own conceit"* (Proverbs 18:11; 26:6, 12, 16; 18:11; Romans 11:25, 12:16), and in Proverbs 3:7, *"Do not be wise in your own eyes."*

God tells us that self-control is "the fruit of the Spirit."

2. To control fleshly lusts which war against the soul, dependence must be on the Spirit

"Let no one being tempted say, I am tempted from God. For God is not tempted by evils, and He tempts no one. But each one is tempted by his own lusts, having been drawn out and having been seduced [by them]. Then being conceived, lust brings forth sin. And sin fully formed brings forth death" (James 1:13-15).

The lusts of the flesh are many, so many that one lust wars against another:

"From where [are] wars and fightings among you. [Is it] not from this, from your lusts warring in your members?" (James 4:1).

3. There is a scriptural solution to controlling self-indulgence

"But He gives greater grace. Because of this it says, God sets [Himself] against proud ones, but He gives grace to humble ones. Then be subject to God. Resist the Devil, and he will flee from you" (James 4:6; Proverbs 3:34)

The Spirit gives a solution in the words He breathed out. And these holy words may be successfully used against the world, the flesh, and the Devil. Those who have *"the mind . . . which also was in Christ Jesus,"* (Philippians 2:5); who have *"the mind of the Spirit"* and are *"led by the Spirit,"* (Romans 8:6, 14), these are *"the ones belonging to Christ"* and it is said that these have *"crucified the flesh with [its] passions and lusts"* The persons who have such a mind will have self-control, so that they will be able to restrain their fleshly lusts and passions.

> *"bringing in all diligence, filling in your faith [with] virtue; and virtue [with] knowledge; and knowledge [with] self-control; and self-control [with] patience; and patience [with] godliness; and godliness [with] brotherly love; and brotherly love [with] love"* (2 Peter 1:5-7)

The importance of maintaining self-control can be seen by noticing how the Spirit links this together with other prime graces.

4. Those who refuse to take heed to Scripture warnings are doomed:

> *"For from within, out of the heart of men, pass out the evil thoughts, adulteries, fornications, murders, thefts, greedy desires, iniquities, deceit, lustful desires, a wicked eye, blasphemy, pride, foolishness. All these things pass out from within and defile the man"* (Mark 7:21-23)

> *"Therefore, to [anyone] knowing to do good, and not doing [it], it is sin to him"* (James 4:17)

In chapter 1 of Romans, God tells us that the universe reveals the Godhead, leaving all persons on earth guilty, *"for them to be without excuse"* (Romans 1:20)

But also it has been written:

> *"[The] Lord knows to deliver the godly out of temptation, and to keep the unjust for a day of judgment, being punished"* (2 Peter 2:9)

Those who are content to be unjust will still be unjust on Judgment Day (Revelation 22:11). Those who have the Spirit lusting against their flesh will not be content to be intemperate, but will strive in that strength which the faithful God has promised,

"who will not allow you to be tempted above what you are able, but with the temptation [He] will also make the way out, so that you may be able to bear [it]"

This applies to self-control, as well as to any other temptation that may threaten a saint of God. The newborn children of God will be careful to learn to discipline themselves, being guided by the Spirit to gain self-control through reading of the Scriptures through and through.

S. Comfort and encouragement

1. God the Father is the prime source of comfort and encouragement.

"desiring to more fully declare to the heirs of the promise the unchangeableness of His counsel, God interposed by an oath, that through two unchangeable things in which [it was] not possible [for] God to lie, we might have a strong consolation, those who have fled to lay hold on the hope set before [us] which we have as an anchor of the soul, both certain and sure, and entering into the inner [side] of the veil, where Jesus entered as forerunner for us" (Hebrews 6:17-20a)

Whatever the trials, troubles, temptations, stresses, anxieties that occur to the saints, God consoles them with numerous promises of relief, and even joy (James 1:2-4).

For an example, wisdom to cope is positively offered to one who asks.

"But if any of you lacks wisdom, let him ask from God, [who] gives to all freely and with no reproach, and it will

46

be given to Him. But let him ask in faith, doubting noth-
ing . . . " (James 1: 5, 6)

2. Our God and Savior, Jesus Christ, is a fountain of much comfort.

"Now may our Lord Jesus Christ Himself, and our God and Father, the [One] having loved us, and having given us everlasting comfort and a good hope by grace, may He comfort your hearts and establish you in every good word and work" (2 Thessalonians 2:16,17)

With great confidence the apostle Paul prayed that the Thessalonians would have everlasting comfort and good hope, which would establish them in *"every good word and work."* This comfort is available to all who seek it in the name of the Lord Jesus Christ.

"But immediately Jesus spoke to them, Be comforted! I AM!" (Matthew 14:27)

Fourteen times in the New Testament Jesus identified Himself as the great I AM. That is, He was saying, I am God, for He is referring back to Exodus 3:13 where He as the Jehovah who dealt with Moses in the wilderness gave this name to Himself, *"I AM THAT I AM."* The Jews knew that when He declared to them I AM, this is what He was saying, for they condemned Him for saying I AM in that infamous trial, charging Him with blasphemy because He was saying He was God (Mark 14:62; Luke 22:70). Another time they took up stones to stone Him for saying I AM! (John. 8:58). He called that His name (Luke 21:8). And He said I AM! when He had just performed the miracle of walking on the water (Matthew 14:27). Three times He told the mob that He was God when they had come to arrest Him, saying, I AM! (John 18:5, 6, 8). See also Mark 13:6; John 4:26; 8:24, 28, 13:19. It was a great comfort to His sheep, but a great disturbance to all others when He declared that He was God by saying I AM!

47

3. The Holy Spirit of God has the name of "the Comforter"

"But I tell you the truth, it is profitable for you that I should go away. For if I do not go away, the Comforter [the Holy Spirit] will not come to you" (John 16:7)

There are a multitude of ways that God the Spirit is a comfort to the saints. He is the One who guides the children of God into all truth:

"But when that One comes, He will guide you into all truth" (John 16:13)

Then there are the wonderful fruits of the Spirit which are a comfort and consolation to His people:

"But the fruit of the Spirit is love, peace, long-suffering, kindness, goodness, faith, meekness, self-control." (Galatians 5:22, 23)

In the Scriptures alone are found any comfort worthy of the name.

T. Riches, treasure and wealth

1. God owns everything, and He gives it to whomever He desires

"The silver [is] Mine, and the gold [is] Mine, says Jehovah of hosts" [Haggai 2:8]

Whatever kind of riches there are, they all belong to God, the silver, the gold, and the cattle on a thousand hills (Psalm 50:10), as well as all heavenly treasures. Those who have earthly riches are but stewards of God for the short time they are here (or it may be that they will have them an even shorter time, for wealth *"flies away [into] the heavens like the eagle"* (Proverbs 23:5).

2. Riches may be a stumbling block, or at least a cause of dissatisfaction.

Many are those who have found riches and wealth the cause of a very evil effect on their lives. Among these was the man who was called the wisest man on earth, Solomon. Oh how great was his fall!

"He who loves silver will not be satisfied with silver, and he who loves abundance does not gain. This [is] also vanity" (Ecclesiastes 5:10)

"One trusting in his riches, he shall fall; but like a green leaf the righteous shall sprout" (Proverbs 11:28)

King Agur even prayed that God would not give him riches, lest he become full and deceive, saying, *"Who is Jehovah?"* (Proverbs 30:8)

3. Riches and wealth are not the best things, even on this earth.

One of the greatest lessons that can be learned about life while on this earth is the fact that God holds out to us blessings that are far more precious than earthbound things.

"Wisdom [is] more precious than rubies, and all the things you can desire are not to be compared with her. Length of days [is] in her right hand, riches and honor in her left hand" (Proverbs 3:15, 16)

Another man who at the time perhaps was the richest man on earth, a most admired and godly man, denied that he had made a god of his riches: He is noted in the Bible for two other qualities, his integrity (Job 1:8; 2:3) and his patience (James 5:11). Job denies that he put any trust in his riches:
"If I have made gold my hope or have called fine gold my trust; if I rejoiced because my wealth [was] great, or

because my hand had gotten much, . . . this also [would be] an iniquity [for] the judges, for I would have denied God above" (Job 31:24,25, 28).

And it is also written:

"Come now rich ones, weep, howling over your miseries coming on. Your riches have rotted, and your garments have become come moth-eaten. Your gold and silver have rotted over, and their poison will be a testimony to you, and will eat your flesh as fire . . . " (James 5:1-3)

4. There is a safe and enduring place where one can store up treasure.

"Do not treasure up for you treasures on the earth, where moth and rust cause to vanish, and where thieves dig through and steal. But treasure up for you treasures in Heaven, where neither moth nor rust cause to vanish, and where thieves do not dig through and steal. For where your treasure is, there your heart will be also" (Matthew 6:19-21)

In the Scriptures one learns what true treasure is, and where to store it.

U. Guidance and direction in your life

1. God the Holy Spirit is the guide who administers the decrees of God:

"And there are differences of workings, but the same God is working all things in all. And to each one is given the showing forth of the Spirit to [our] profit" (1 Corinthians 12:6, 7)

Whether it is the work of regeneration, the giving of a word of wisdom, or faith and the other fruits of the Spirit, of healing, of powers, of prophecy, of One who bore along the writers of the Scriptures, it is written:

"But the one and the same Spirit works all these things, distributing separately to each as He wills" (1 Corinthians 12:11)

It is in the Word of truth that this guidance is provided, as well as in direct inworking of the indwelling Spirit to remind one of what it says.

"He [God the Holy Spirit] *will guide you into all truth."* (John 16:13)

When one's prayers are beyond words, the Spirit joins in to help us by pleading our cause:

"And likewise the Spirit also joins in to help our weaknesses. For we do not know what we should pray as we ought, but the Spirit Himself pleads our cause for us with groanings that cannot be uttered" (Romans 8:26)

2. The Holy Spirit is the divine Person who administers providence

"O Jehovah, I know that his way does not [belong] to man; [it is] not in man who walks to direct his steps" (Jeremiah 10:23)

God affirms this right, this divine prerogative to direct the steps of every person. Otherwise, how could He cause His eternal decrees to come to pass?

"Trust in Jehovah with all your heart, and lean not to your own understanding; in all your ways acknowledge Him, and He will direct your steps" (Proverbs 3:5, 6)

(A) Positively, leaning to one's own understanding is a hindrance to having God-directed steps that are a blessing.

(B) Negatively, no one can have have the ability to deny God's right to direct him:

"The steps of a man are ordered from Jehovah . . ." (Psalm 37:23)

"A man's heart plans his way, but Jehovah fixes his step" (Proverbs 16:9)

From this power and authority God could determine the Scriptures to be written, every word of them, and all the words of them, so that with certainty His children could be instructed and encouraged that He could and would make *"all things work together for good to those who love God, to those who are the called according to [His] purpose"* (Romans 8:28).

3. By nature everyone prefers to trust in his or her own wisdom

"There is a way that seems right to a man, but the end of it [is] the ways of death" (Proverbs 14:12)

Thanks be to God that He has the right, the wisdom, and the power to overrule man's choices:

"Many purposes are in a man's heart, but the counsel of Jehovah shall stand" (Proverbs 19:21).

How thankful should God's children be that it is His counsel that shall stand.

4. God has given His Word that the ones believing into Christ will have everlasting life

"Truly, truly, I say to you, the [one] believing into Me has everlasting life" (John 6:47)

"But these have been written that you may believe that Jesus is the Christ, the Son of God, and that believing you

may have life in His name" (John 20:31 - see also John 3:16, 36; 5:24)

The purposes of God will be fulfilled minutely, whether to give everlasting life to His chosen *"vessels of mercy"* (Romans 9:23), or everlasting condemnation to His *"vessels of wrath"* (Romans 9:22). God gives guidance and direction through His Word:

"So shall My Word be which goes out of My mouth. It shall not return to Me void, but it shall accomplish that which I please, and it shall prosper in what I sent it to do!" (Isaiah 55:11)

To anyone to whom God has given the opportunity to read the Scriptures, it would be the height of foolishness for such a person to ignore the words that gives guidance how to escape everlasting punishment in the *"Hell of fire"* (Mark 9:47)

. . . where their worm does not die, and the fire is not put out" (Mark 9:46)

"For what things were written were written for our instruction, that through patience and encouragement of the Scriptures we might have hope" (Romans 15:5)

V. Full knowledge of the truth is in Jesus

1. Since Jesus is "the Truth," full knowledge must come through Him

To have full knowledge of the truth, one must know Jesus who is *""the Truth."* (John 14:6)

But you have not so learned Jesus, if indeed you heard Him and were taught in Him, as the truth [is] in Jesus" (Ephesians 4:20, 21)

For this reason the Scriptures emphasize the necessity of hearing and being taught by Him, who speaks to men through the Spirit of God and His God-breathed Words:

"I am the Way, the Truth, and the Life" (John 14:6)

To whom else could we go for full knowledge of the truth, than to Jesus, who exhorts us:

"If you continue in My Word you are truly My disciples, and you will know the truth, and the truth will set your free" (John 8:31, 32)

2. There being but one God, God the Spirit is also said to be "the truth"

"And the Spirit is the [One] witnessing, because the Spirit is the truth" (1 John 5:6)

Since the Spirit of God is the Author of the Scriptures, He is the One who guides believers into all truth. And all truth is in those same Scriptures:

"Your Word is truth" (John 17:17)

3. Nothing is more important to any one than studying and knowing God's Word

Among his last words in the Scriptures the apostle John warns us that we must know the truth and practice it:

"If we say that we have fellowship with Him, and we walk in the darkness, we lie and are not practicing the truth" (1 John 1:6)

"If we say that we have no sin, we deceive ourselves, and the truth is not in us" (1 John 1:8)

And the apostle Peter's wrote these words, as he was *"borne along by [the] Holy Spirit:"* (2 Peter 1:21):

"For these things being in you, and abounding, [they will] make you not idle, not unfruitful in the full knowledge of our Lord Jesus Christ" (2 Peter 1:8)

And Peter's last words in the Scriptures urged all the saints:
"But grow in grace and knowledge of our Lord and Savior, Jesus Christ. To Him [be] the glory, both now and to [the] day of eternity" (2 Peter 3:18).

W. Safety

1. Safety and security rest in God

Only in God is safety: To be saved from straits, fear, or any variety of evils, to God one must go:
"I will both lie down in peace and sleep, for You alone, O Jehovah, make me dwell in safety" (Psalm 4:8)

"Turn to Me and be saved, all the ends of the earth; for I [am] God, and there [is] no other" (Isaiah 45:22):

2. God governs the safety of all through His providence

Before they cried, He answered, because He had providentially arranged the situation and moved all parties so that their safety was secured.
"and they cried to Jehovah in their distress; He saved them from their straits" (Psalm 107:19)

3. Many times it is God the Son as Jehovah that guarantees safety.

In the Proverbs, chapters 1 and 8, Wisdom is personification of God the Son, and it is His promises that ease from dread:

"But he who listens to Me (Wisdom) shall live securely, and shall be at ease from the dread of evil" (Proverbs 1:33)

4. Many times God's nearness is connected to character

In the Bible there are many verses that teach that there is a nearness of God to those who are broken-hearted, contrite, lowly, and humble. We learn that there are many advantages open to those of a broken heart and contrite spirit:

"My defense [is] on God, who saves the upright in heart" (Psalm 7:10).

"Jehovah [is] near those who [are] broken-hearted, and saves those who have a contrite spirit. Many are the evils of the righteous, but Jehovah helps him out of them all" (Psalm 34:18, 19)

A more humbling verse would be hard to find. Imagine seeking safety in any other when it is known that God is dwelling within one.

"I dwell in the high and lofty place, even with the contrite and humble of spirit; to make live the spirit of the humble and to make live the heart of the contrite ones" (Isaiah 57:15)

X. Help

1. God alone can be trusted to help the godly

There is only One who can be trusted to come to the help of the godly in time of need, the one and only God, there is no other.

"God [is] our refuge and strength, very much found [to be] a help in distresses" (Psalm 46:1)

"Turn to Me and be saved, all the ends of the earth; for I [am] God, and there [is] no other" (Isaiah 45:22)

2. God the Spirit is sensitive to the needs of the elect

Whether in weakness, in prayer, or distress, the Spirit pleads our case:

"And likewise the Spirit also joins in to help our weaknesses. For we do not know what we should pray as we ought, but the Spirit Himself pleads our case for us with groanings that cannot be uttered" (Romans 8:26)

"So that we may confidently say, [The] Lord is my helper, and I will not be afraid; what can man do to me" (Hebrews 13:6; Psalm 118:6)

When God is one's help, He makes even the weak strong, and will confound those who fight you:

"Do not fear, for I [am] with you. Do not gaze about, for I [am] your God; I have made you strong. Yea, I helped you; yes, I uphold you with the right hand of My righteousness. Behold! All who were provoked with you are ashamed and confounded; they are as nothing; and they who fight with you are perishing" (Isaiah 41:10, 11)

3. Even weakness attracts God's grace and strength

The apostle Paul prayed for relief, but it was not given to him to have the specific kind of relief that he had asked. God's grace is always sufficient, and He is an ever-present Helper to all His children, yet He decides the how, the when, and the where His provision shall be.

"And He said to me, My grace is sufficient for you, for My power is perfected in weakness" (2 Corinthians 12:9).

Otherwise He could not make *"all things work together for our good to those who love God, [to] those who are called according to [His] purpose"* (Romans 8:28)

Y. Fruitfulness

1. God the Son chose those who would go and bear fruit

The lambs of Christ cannot bear fruit unless they abide in Him,

"You have not chosen Me, but I chose you out and planted you, that you should go and should bear fruit, and your fruit abide . . ." (John 15:16)

"the [one] abiding in Me, and I in him, this one bears much fruit" (John 15:4).

In his commentary John Trapp (TCNT) comments on this verse, "All our sap and safety is from Christ. The bud of a good desire, the blossom of a good resolution, and the fruit of a good action, all come from Him"

2. God the Spirit generates lives that bear fruit

From where do these fruits originate? As is true of all good things, they are from God (James 1:17). It is the role of God the Spirit to nourish the children of God so that they will bear much spiritual fruit.

"For the fruit of the Spirit [is] in all goodness, and righteousness, and truth" (Ephesians 5:9).

"So that, my brothers, you also were made dead to the law through the body of Christ, for you to become Another's, to [One] raised from [the] dead, so that we may bear fruit to God" (Romans 7:4)

58

3. Essentially, directions for fruit bearing are to be found throughout God's Word

Many of the fruits God's grace gives to the godly are mentioned in the Scriptures:

"Because of the hope being laid up for you in Heaven, which you heard before in the Word of truth of the gospel, coming to you . . . and it is bearing fruit even also among you" (Colossians 1:5)

"The fruits of righteousness" (2 Corinthians 9:10; Philippians 1:11); *"the fruit of your lips,"* (Hebrews 13:15), such as prayer, thanksgiving. *Love, joy, peace, longsuffering, gentleness, goodness, faith, meekness are all called "the fruit of the Spirit"* (Galatians 5:22, 23).

All the saints have these fruits, and they are expected to develop them, and then to display them to others.

4. There are fruits of men that lead to destruction

Those who bear no fruit are identified as ones for whom the fires of Hell are reserved

"And have no fellowship with the unfruitful works of darkness, but rather even reprove [them]. (Ephesians 5:11)

"These are those being sown into the thorn bushes, those having heard the Word, and the anxieties of the age, and the deceitfulness of riches about other things entering in, [they] choke the Word, and it becomes unfruitful" (Mark 4:18, 19)

If the *"root of the matter,"* (Job 19:28), the fruits of the Spirit, are not displayed in the thoughts and actions of a person, they are *"twice dead"* (Jude 12), *"dead while living"* (1 Timothy 5:6). Out of the heart of such flow those fruits of darkness which are described in Mark 7:21, 22. With such the saints are not to have fellowship, lest they become defiled or desensitized by them..

"by their fruits you shall know them" (Matthew 7:20; 1 Corinthians 6:17).

Z. Divine warnings

There are many warnings in the Scriptures that enable you to avoid the pitfalls that lurk for you in *"the body of this death"* which you must carry with you until that Day *"when all things are subjected to Him"* (Romans 7:24; 1 Corinthians 15:25-27)

Warning 1. The Holy Spirit is the difference between life and death

The Word of God teaches how one can *"put to death the practices of the body"* (Romans 8:13). This is accomplished by the Holy Spirit, *"through the indwelling of His Spirit in you"*(Romans 8:11).

"But if Christ [is] in you, the body indeed [is] dead because of sin, but the Spirit [is] life because of righteousness. But if the Spirit of the [One] having raised Jesus from [the] dead dwells in you, the [One] having raised the Christ from [the] dead will also make your mortal bodies live through the indwelling of the Spirit" (Romans 8:10, 11)

Once these inescapable facts have been made known to a sinner, surely there will follow a search of the Word of God to learn how one can live and not die.

"For if you live according to flesh, you are going to die. But if by [the} Spirit ... you will live" (Romans 8:13)

Warning 2. All without Christ are dead

Those believing into Christ will rise from the dead because of the resurrection of Christ from the dead. All others *"being by nature the children of wrath"* will suffer everlasting punishment in the fires of Hell for their sins, *"where their worm does not die, and the fire is not put out"* (Mark 9:48, Isaiah 66:24)

By nature the children of God were the children of wrath:
For they *"were once dead in trespasses and sins, in which"* [they] *"then walked according to the course of this world, according to the ruler of the authority of the air, the spirit now working in the sons of disobedience, among whom we also all conducted ourselves formerly in the lusts of our flesh, doing the things willed of the flesh and of the understandings, and were by nature the children of wrath, even as the rest"*(Ephesians 2:1-3)

But God was rich in mercy toward His *"vessels of mercy"* (Romans 9:23):

"But God being rich in mercy, because of the great love [with] which He loved us, even we being dead in sins, [He] made us alive together with Christ; by grace you are being saved" (Ephesians 2:4, 5).

Warning 3. Those without the Spirit of God indwelling them must beware:

Warnings against all kinds of dangers to the reader make up a substantial portion of Holy Scripture. The philosophies, illogic, and deceitfulness of fallen mankind are an ever-present source of woe to God's children.

"Watch that there not be one robbing you through philosophy and empty deceit, according to the tradition of men, according to the elements of the world, and not according

to Christ, for in Him dwells all the fullness of the Godhead bodily" (Colossians 2:8, 9)

"And He said to them, Beware, and keep back from covetousness, for one's life is not in the abundance of the things which are his" (Luke 12:15)

The way of the Cross is the only remedy for the ravages of warring lusts in the breast of mankind. And nowhere may the warnings and the remedies to the dangers be found except in the Bible. For working with His Word, the Spirit gives the spiritual strength and character to persist in conquering them:

"Do not love the world, nor the things in the world. If anyone loves the world the love of the Father is not in him, because all [that is] in the world the lust of the flesh, the lust of the eyes, and the pride of life, is not of the Father, but is of the world (1 John 2:15, 16)

It is a moment by moment, hour by hour, day by day, year by year vigilance that is needed, because *"the days are evil."* Blank minds, idle minds, passive minds and idle hands are the devil's playground.

The saints must redeem the time by studying God's Word, meditating upon it, and applying it to their daily lives. By this means they will develop a Biblical approach to life, a world-view that will protect against lapses in watchfulness.

"Then watch how carefully you walk, not as unwise, but as wise ones, redeeming the time, because the days are evil (Ephesian 5:15, 16).

OUR PRAYER FOR YOU

Beloved reader, remember that it is written: ***"Truly, truly, I say to you, everyone practicing sin is a slave of sin"*** (John 8:34).

Speaking through the Word of God, Jesus says to you:

"If I had not come and spoken to them, they had no sin. But now they do not have excuse concerning sin" (John 15:22)

And through the Apostle James, God the Spirit warns:

"to [anyone] knowing to do good, and not doing [it[, it is sin to him" (James 4:17)

Our prayer for you is that which the Apostle Peter spoke as his last words in the Scriptures:

"Then, beloved, you knowing beforehand, watch lest being led away by the error of the lawless you fall from [your] steadfastness. But grow in grace and knowledge of our Lord and Savior, Jesus Christ. To Him being the glory, both now and to [the] day of eternity. Amen." (2 Peter 3:17, 18).

What is written in the law? How readest thou?

READER,

The question before your eyes is 1800 years old. It was asked by our Lord Jesus Christ. It was asked concerning the Bible.

I invite you to examine and consider this question. I warn you, it is just as mighty and important now as it was on the day when it came from our Lord's lips. I want to apply it to the conscience of every one who reads this paper, and to knock at the door of his heart. I would fain sound a trumpet in the ear of every one who speaks English, and cry aloud, "How readest thou? Dost thou read the Bible?"

Why do I hold this question to be of such mighty importance? Why do I press it on the notice of every man, as a matter of life and death? Give me your attention for a few minutes, and you shall see. Follow me through these pages, and you shall hear why I ask, "HOW READEST THOU? DOST THOU READ THE BIBLE?"

I. I ask, first of all, because *there is no knowledge absolutely needful to a man's salvation, except a knowledge of the things which are to be found in the Bible.*

We live in days when the words of Daniel are fulfilled before our eyes: "Many run to and fro, and knowledge is increased" (Daniel 12:4). Schools are multiplying on every side. New colleges are set up. Old universities are reformed and improved. New books are continually coming forth. More is being taught, more is being learned, more is being read, than there ever was since the world began. It is all well. I rejoice at it. An ignorant population is a perilous and expensive burden to any nation. It is a ready prey to the first Absalom, or Catiline, or Wat Tyler, or Jack Cade, who may arise to entice it to do evil.[1] But this I say— we must never forget that all the education a man's head can receive will not save his soul from hell, unless he knows the truths of the Bible.

A man *may have prodigious learning, and yet never be saved*. He may be master of half the languages spoken round the globe. He may be acquainted with the highest and deepest things in heaven and earth. He may have read books till he is like a walking cyclopædia. He may be familiar with the stars of heaven, the birds of the air, the beasts of the earth, and the fishes of the sea. He may be able, like Solomon, to "speak of trees, from the cedar of Lebanon to the hyssop that grows on the wall, of beasts also, and fowls, and creeping things, and fishes" (1 Kings 4:33). He may be able to discourse of all the secrets of fire, air, earth, and water. And yet, if he dies ignorant of Bible truths, he dies a miserable man. Chemistry never silenced a guilty conscience. Mathematics never healed a broken heart. All the sciences in the world never smoothed down a dying pillow. No earthly philosophy ever supplied hope in death. No natural theology ever gave peace in the prospect of meeting a holy God. All these things are of the earth, earthy, and can never raise a man above the earth's level. They may enable a man to strut and fret his little season here below with a more dignified gait than his fellow mortals, but they can never give him wings, and enable him to soar towards heaven. He that has the largest share of them will find at length that without Bible knowledge he has got no lasting possession. Death will make an end of all his attainments, and after death they will do him no good at all.

A man *may be a very ignorant man, and yet be saved*. He may be unable to read a word, or write a letter. He may know nothing of geography beyond the bounds of his own parish, and be utterly unable to say which is nearest, Paris or New York. He may know nothing of arithmetic, and not see any difference between a mil-

[1] All four were leaders of failed rebellions: Absalom against King David (2 Samuel 15—18); Catiline (d. 62 b.c.) against the late Roman Republic; Wat Tyler (d. 1381) against Richard II; and Jack Cade (d. 1450) against Henry VI.

lion and a thousand. He may know nothing of history, not even of his own land, and be quite ignorant whether his country owes most to Semiramis, Boadicea, or Queen Elizabeth.[1] He may know nothing of the affairs of his own times, and be incapable of telling you whether the Chancellor of the Exchequer, or the Commander-in-Chief, or the Archbishop of Canterbury is managing the national finances. He may know nothing of science and its discoveries: and whether Julius Cæsar won his victories by gunpowder, or the apostles had a printing press, or the sun goes round the earth, may be matters about which he has not an idea. And yet if that very man has heard Bible truth with his ears, and believed it with his heart, he knows enough to save his soul. He will be found at last with Lazarus in Abraham's bosom, while his scientific fellow-creature, who has died unconverted, is lost forever.

Knowledge of the Bible, in short, is the one knowledge that is needful. A man may get to heaven without money, learning, health, or friends—but without Bible knowledge he will never get there at all. A man may have the mightiest of minds, and a memory stored with all that mighty mind can grasp—and yet, if he does not know the things of the Bible, he will make shipwreck of his soul forever. Woe! woe! woe to the man who dies in ignorance of the Bible!

Reader, this is the Book about which I am addressing you today. It is no light matter *what you do with such a book*. It concerns the life of your soul. I summon you—I charge you to give an honest answer to my question. What art thou doing with the Bible? Dost thou read it? How readest thou?

II. I ask, in the second place, because *there is no book in existence written in such a manner as the Bible.*

The Bible is "given by inspiration of God" (2 Timothy 3:16). In this respect it is utterly unlike all other writings. God taught the writers of it what to say. God put into their minds thoughts and

---

[1] Semiramis was a legendary ninth-century B.C. Assyrian queen; Boadicea was an ancient British queen (d. A.D. 60); and Queen Elizabeth (1533–1603) was the first Protestant Queen of England.

ideas. God guided their pens in setting down those thoughts and ideas. When you read it, you are not reading the self-taught compositions of poor imperfect men like yourself, but the words of the eternal God. When you hear it, you are not listening to the erring opinions of short-lived mortals, but to the unchanging mind of the King of kings. The men who were employed to indite the Bible "spake not of themselves." They "spake as they were moved by the Holy Ghost." (2 Peter 1:21.) All other books in the world, however good and useful in their way, are more or less defective. The more you look at them, the more you see their defects and blemishes. The Bible alone is absolutely perfect. From beginning to end it is "the Word of God."

I shall not waste time by attempting any long and laboured proof of this. I say boldly that the Book itself is the best witness of its own inspiration. It is utterly inexplicable and unaccountable in any other point of view. It is the greatest standing miracle in the world. He that dares to say the Bible is not inspired, let him give a reasonable account of it, if he can. Let him explain the history and character of the Book in a way that will satisfy any man of common sense. The burden of proof seems to my mind to lie on him. I shall content myself with stating some plain facts about the Bible, which can neither be denied nor explained away. And the ground I shall take up is this, that these facts ought to satisfy every reasonable inquirer that the Bible is of God, and not of man. They are simple facts, which require no knowledge of Hebrew, or Greek, or Latin, in order to be understood; yet they are facts which prove to my own mind conclusively that the Bible is superhuman, or not of man.

(a) It is a fact that there is an *extraordinary unity and harmony in the contents of the Bible*, which is entirely above man. We all know how difficult it is to get a story told by any three persons, not living together, in which there are not some contradictions and discrepancies. If the story is a long one, and involves a large quantity of particulars, unity seems almost impossible among the common run of men. But it is not so with the Bible. Here is a book written by not less than thirty different persons. The writers were men of every rank and class in society. One was a lawgiver. One was a warlike king. One was a peaceful king. One was a herdsman. One had been brought up as a publican, another as a physician, another as a learned Pharisee, two as fishermen, several as priests. They lived at different intervals, over a space of 1500 years; and the greater part of them never saw each other face to face. And yet there is a perfect harmony among all these writers. They all write as if they were under one dictation. The handwriting may vary, but the mind that runs through their work is always one and the same. They all tell the same story. They all give one account of man, one account of God, one account of the way of salvation, one account of the heart. You see truth unfolding under their hands, as you go through the volume of their writings—but you never detect any real contradiction, or contrariety of view.

I ask my readers to mark this fact, and ponder it well. Tell me not that this unity might be the result of chance. The man who can believe *that* must indeed be a credulous person. There is only one satisfactory account of the Book. The Bible is not of man, but of God. *It was written under the direct inspiration of God.*

(b) It is another fact that there is an *extraordinary accuracy in the facts and statements of the Bible, which is above man.* Here is a book that has been finished and before the world for more than 1800 years. These 1800 years have been the busiest and most changeful period the world has ever seen. During this period the greatest discoveries have been made in science, the greatest alterations in the ways and customs of society, the greatest improvements in the habits and usages of life. Hundreds of things might be named which satisfied and pleased our fore-fathers, which we have laid aside long ago as obsolete, useless, and old-fashioned. The laws, the books, the houses, the furni-ture, the clothes, the carriages of each succeeding century, have been a continual improvement on those of the century that went before. There is hardly a work of brain or hands in which faults and weak points have not been discovered. There is hardly an institution which has not gone through a process of sifting, purifying, refining, simplifying, reforming, amending, and changing. But all this time men have never discovered a weak point or a defect in the Bible. Infidels have assailed it in vain. There it stands—perfect, and fresh, and complete—as it did eighteen centuries ago. The march of intellect never overtakes it. The wisdom of wise men never gets beyond it. The science of philosophers never proves it wrong. The discoveries of travellers never convict it of mistakes. Are the distant islands of the Pacific laid open? Nothing is found that in the slightest degree contradicts the Bible account of man's heart. Are the ruins of Nineveh and Egypt ransacked and explored? Nothing is found that overturns one jot or tittle of the Bible's historical statements. On the contrary, they are continually receiving fresh confirmation. How shall we account for this fact? Who could have thought it possible that so large a book, handling such a vast variety of subjects, should, at the end of these years, be found so free from erroneous statements? There is only one satisfactory account to be given of the fact. The Bible was *written by inspiration of God.*

(c) It is another fact that there is an *extraordinary wisdom, sublimity, and majesty in the style of the Bible,* which is above man. Strange and unlikely as it was, the writers of Scripture have produced a book which even at this day is utterly unrivalled. With all our boasted attainments in science and art and learning, we can produce nothing in literature that can be compared with the Bible. Even at this very hour, in the nineteenth century, the Book stands entirely alone. No other book in existence comes near it. There is a strain and a style and a tone of thought about it, which separate it from all other writings. There are no weak points, and motes, and flaws, and blemishes. There is no mixture of infirmity and feebleness, such as you will find in the works of even the best Christians. "Holy, holy, holy,"[1] seems written on every page. To talk of comparing the Bible with other "sacred books" so-called, such as the Koran, the Shasters, or the Book of Mormon is positively absurd. You might as well compare the sun with a rushlight, or Mount Blanc with a molehill, or St. Paul's with an Irish hovel, or the Portland Vase with a garden pot, or

[1] Isaiah 6:3; Revelation 4:8.

the Koh-i-noor diamond with a bit of glass.[1] God seems to have allowed the existence of these pretended revelations in order to prove the immeasurable superiority of His own Word. To talk of the inspiration of the Bible as only differing *in degree* from that of such writings as the works of Homer, Plato, Shakespeare, Danté, and Milton is simply a piece of blasphemous folly. Every honest and unprejudiced reader must see that there is a gulf between the Bible and any other book, which no man can fathom. You feel at turning from the Scriptures to other works that you have got into a new atmosphere. You feel like one who has exchanged gold for base metal, and heaven for earth. And how can this mighty difference be accounted for? The men who wrote the Bible had no special advantages. They lived in a remote corner of the civilized earth. They had, most of them, little leisure, few books, and no learning—such as learning is reckoned in this world. Yet the Book they composed is one which is unrivalled! There is but one way of accounting for this fact. *They wrote under the direct inspiration of God.*

(*d*) It is another fact that there is in the Bible an extraordinary *suitableness to the spiritual wants of all mankind*. It exactly meets the heart of man in every rank or class, in every country and climate, in every age and period of life. It is the only book in existence which is never out of place and out of date. Other books after a time become obsolete and old-fashioned. The Bible never does. Other books suit one country or people, and not another. The Bible suits all. It is the Book of the poor and unlearned, no less than of the rich and the philosopher. It feeds the mind of the labourer in his cottage, and it satisfies the gigantic intellects of Chalmers, Brewster, and Faraday.[2] Lord

[1] Mount Blanc is the highest peak in the Alps (15,771 feet); St. Paul's Cathedral, London, is a universally known landmark of the City; the Portland Vase is a first-century A.D. vase considered the finest surviving Roman example of cameo glass; and the Koh-i-noor (Persian, "Mountain of Light") diamond is a magnificent stone, weighing 109 carats, which was placed among the crown jewels of Queen Victoria.

[2] Thomas Chalmers (1780–1847), Sir David Brewster (1781–1868), Michael Faraday (1791–1867), were scientific geniuses, whose minds were captive to the Scriptures.

Macaulay, and John Bright,[1] and the writers of brilliant articles in the *Times*, and the humblest city missionaries are all under obligations to the same volume. It is equally valued by the converted New Zealander in the southern hemisphere, and the Red River Indian in the cold north of America, and the Hindoo under the tropical sun.

It is the only book, moreover, which seems always fresh and ever green and new. For eighteen centuries it has been studied and prayed over by millions of private Christians, and expounded and explained and preached to us by thousands of ministers. Fathers, and schoolmen, and Reformers, and Puritans, and modern divines have incessantly dug down into the mine of Scripture, and yet never exhausted it. It is a well never dry, and a field which is never barren. It meets the hearts and minds and consciences of Christians in the nineteenth century as fully as it did those of Greeks and Romans when it was first completed. It suits the "dairyman's daughter" as well as Persis, or Tryphena, or Tryphosa[2]—and the English peer as well as the converted African at Sierra Leone. It is still the first book which fits the child's mind when he begins to learn religion, and the last to which the old man clings as he leaves the world. In short, it suits all ages, ranks, climates, minds, conditions. It is the one book which suits the world.

Now how shall we account for this singular fact? What satisfactory explanation can we give? There is only one account and explanation. The Bible was *written by divine inspiration*. It is the book of the world, because He inspired it who formed the world, who made all nations of one blood, and knows man's common nature. It is the book for every heart, because He dictated it who alone knows all hearts, and what all hearts require. *It is the Book of God.*

---

[1] Thomas Macaulay (1800–1859) and John Bright (1811–1889) were British political reformers; both are remembered for their eloquent statesmanship and evangelical piety.

[2] *The Dairyman's Daughter* was the title of a nineteenth-century bestseller, which chronicled the extraordinary life, conversion, and untimely death of a very ordinary Welsh maid, Elizabeth Wallbridge (1770–1801); Persis, Tryphena, and Tryphosa are three women named in Scripture of whom we only know they served the Lord Jesus Christ (Romans 16:12).

It proves nothing against inspiration, as some have asserted, that the writers of the Bible have each a different style. Isaiah does not write like Jeremiah, and Paul does not write like John. This is perfectly true—and yet the works of these men are not a whit less equally inspired. The waters of the sea have many different shades. In one place they look blue, and in another green. And yet the difference is owing to the depth or shallowness of the part we see, or to the nature of the bottom. The water in every case is the same salt sea. The breath of a man may produce different sounds, according to the character of the instrument on which he plays. The flute, the pipe, and the trumpet have each their peculiar note. And yet the breath that calls forth the notes is in each case one and the same. The light of the planets we see in heaven is very various. Mars, and Saturn, and Jupiter have each a peculiar colour. And yet we know that the light of the sun, which each planet reflects, is in each case one and the same. Just in the same way, the books of the Old and New Testaments are all inspired truth, and yet the aspect of that truth varies according to the mind through which the Holy Ghost makes it flow. The handwriting and style of the writers differ enough to prove that each had a distinct individual being; but the Divine Guide who dictates and directs the whole is always one. All is alike inspired. *Every chapter, and verse, and word is from God.*

Set down this fact in your mind, and do not forget it. The extraordinary contents of the Bible are a great fact which can only be explained by admitting its inspiration. Let my reader mark well what I say. It is a simple broad fact that in the matter of *contents*, the Bible stands entirely alone, and no other book is fit to be named in the same day with it.

Oh! that men who are troubled with doubts, and questionings, and sceptical thoughts about inspiration would calmly examine the Bible for themselves! Oh! that they would act on the advice which was the first step to Augustine's conversion— "Take it up and read it!—take it up and read it!"[1] How many

---

[1] Augustine of Hippo (354–430) was the greatest theologian of the Latin Fathers; the text which led to his conversion was Romans 13:13–14.

Gordian knots[1] this course of action would cut! How many difficulties and objections would vanish away at once, like mist
before the rising sun! How many would soon confess, "The
finger of God is here! God is in this book, and I knew it not."

Reader, this is the Book about which I address you this day.
Surely it is no light matter *what you are doing with this Book.* It is
no light thing that God should have caused this book to be
"written for your learning," and that you should have before you
"the oracles of God" (Romans 15:4; 3:2). I charge you, I summon
you to give an honest answer to my question. What art thou
doing with the Bible? Dost thou read it at all? How READEST
THOU?

III. I ask, in the third place, because *no book in existence contains such important matter as the Bible.*

There is an *extraordinary depth, fulness, and richness in the contents of the Bible.* It throws more light on a vast number of most
important subjects than all the other books in the world put
together. It boldly handles matters which are utterly beyond the
reach of man, when left to himself. It treats of things which are
mysterious and invisible—the soul, the world to come, and
eternity—depths which man has no line to fathom. All who
have tried to write of these things, without Bible light, have
done little but show their own ignorance. They grope like the
blind; they speculate; they guess; they generally make the darkness more visible, and land us in a region of uncertainty and
doubt. How little did the wisest of the heathen know! How dim
were the views of Socrates, Plato, Cicero, and Seneca! A well-
taught Sunday-school child, in the present day, knows more
spiritual truth than all these sages put together.

---

[1] In 333 B.C., Alexander the Great, on his march through Gordium, the
capital of Phrygia, was shown the chariot of the ancient founder of the city,
Gordius, with its yoke lashed to the pole by means of an intricate knot with its
end hidden. According to tradition, this knot was to be untied only by the
future conqueror of Asia; legend says that Alexander sliced through the knot
with his sword. The proverbial phrase "cutting the Gordian knot" has thus
come to denote a bold solution to a complicated problem.

The Bible alone gives a reasonable account of *the beginning and end of the globe on which we live*. It starts from the birthday of the sun, moon, stars, and earth in their present order, and shows us creation in its cradle. It foretells minutely the dissolution of all things—when the stars shall fall from their places, and the earth and all its works shall be burned up—and shows us creation in its grave. It tells us the story of the world's youth, and it tells us the story of its old age. It gives us the picture of its first days, and it gives us the picture of its last. How vast and important is this knowledge!

The Bible alone gives *a true and faithful account of man*. It does not flatter him as novels and romances do. It does not conceal his faults and exaggerate his goodness. It paints him just as he is. It describes him as a fallen creature, very far gone from original righteousness, and of his own nature inclined to evil—a creature needing not only a pardon, but a new heart, to make him fit for heaven. It shows him to be a corrupt being, under every possible circumstance, when left to himself—corrupt after the loss of paradise, corrupt after the flood, corrupt when fenced in by laws and commandments, corrupt when the Son of God visited him as manifest in the flesh, corrupt in the face of warnings, corrupt in the face of miracles, corrupt in the face of judgments, corrupt in the face of mercies. In one word—it shows man to be by nature always a sinner. How important is this knowledge!

The Bible alone gives us *true views of God*. By nature man knows nothing of Him. All his conceptions and ideas of Him are low, grovelling, and debased. What could be more degraded than the gods of the Canaanites and Egyptians—of Babylon, of Greece, and of Rome? What can be more vile than the gods of the Hindoos, and other heathens, in our own times? By the Bible we know that *God hates sin*. The destruction of the world by the flood, the burning of Sodom and Gomorrah, the drowning of Pharaoh and the Egyptians in the Red Sea, the cutting off of the nations of Canaan, the overthrow of Jerusalem and the temple, the scattering of the Jews—all these are unmistakable witnesses. By the Bible we know that *God loves sinners*. His gracious promise in the day of Adam's fall; His longsuffering in the times of Noah; His deliverance of Israel out of the land of Egypt; His gift of the law at Mount Sinai; His bringing the tribes into the promised land; His forbearance in the days of the Judges and Kings; His repeated warnings by the mouth of His prophets; His restoration of Israel after the Babylonian captivity; His sending His Son into the world, in due time, to be crucified; His commanding the gospel to be preached to the Gentiles—all these are speaking facts. By the Bible we learn that *God knows all things*. We see Him foretelling things hundreds and thousands of years before they take place: and as He foretells, so it comes to pass. He foretold that the family of Ham should be a servant of servants, that Tyre should become a rock for drying nets, that Nineveh should become a desolation, that Babylon should be made a desert, that Egypt should be the basest of kingdoms, that Edom should be forsaken and uninhabited, and that the Jews should not be reckoned among the nations. All these things were utterly unlikely and improbable. Yet all have been fulfilled. Reader, once more I say, how vast and important is all this knowledge!

The Bible alone teaches us that *God has made a full, perfect, and complete provision for the salvation of fallen man*. It tells of an atonement made for the sin of the world, by the sacrifice and death of God's own Son upon the cross. It tells us that by His death for sinners, as their Substitute, He has obtained eternal redemption for all that believe on Him. The claims of God's broken law have now been satisfied. "Christ has suffered for sin, the just for the unjust."[1] God can now be just, and yet the justifier of the ungodly. It tells us that there is now a complete remedy for the guilt of sin—even the precious blood of Christ—and peace and rest of conscience for all who believe on Christ. "Whosoever believeth on Him shall not perish, but have eternal life."[2] It tells us that there is a complete remedy for the power of sin—even the almighty grace of the Spirit of Christ. It shows us the Holy Ghost quickening believers, and making them new creatures. It promises a new heart and a new nature to all who will hear

[1] 1 Peter 3:18.   [2] John 3:15.

Christ's voice and follow Him. Reader, once more I say, how important is this knowledge!

The Bible alone *explains the state of things that we see in the world around us.* There are many things on earth which a natural man cannot explain. The amazing inequality of conditions, the poverty and distress, the oppression and persecution, the shakings and tumults, the failures of statesmen and legislators, the constant existence of uncured evils and abuses—all these things are often puzzling to him. He sees, but does not understand. But the Bible makes it all clear. The Bible can tell him that man is a fallen creature, and is of his own nature inclined to evil; that the whole world lieth in wickedness; that the prince of the world, the devil, is everywhere; and that it is vain to look for perfection in the present order of things. The Bible will tell him that neither laws nor education can ever change men's hearts; and that just as no man will ever make a machine work well, unless he allows for friction, so also no man will do much good in the world, unless he always remembers that human nature is fallen, and that the world he works in is full of sin. The Bible will tell him that there is "a good time"[1] certainly coming—and coming perhaps sooner than people expect it—a time of perfect knowledge, perfect justice, perfect happiness, and perfect peace. But the Bible will tell him this time shall not be brought in by any power but that of Christ coming to earth again. And for that second coming of Christ, the Bible will tell him to prepare. Oh! reader, how important is all this knowledge!

But time would fail me, if I were to enter fully into all the great things which the Bible reveals. It is not by any sketch or outline that the treasures of the Bible can be displayed. It would be easy to point out many other things, beside those I have mentioned, and yet the half of its riches would be left untold.

How comforting is the account it gives us of the great Mediator of the New Testament—the man Christ Jesus! Four times over His picture is graciously drawn before our eyes. Four sep-

---

[1] Quoted from "The Good Time Coming," a popular nineteenth-century song, by Charles Mackay (1814–1889).

arate witnesses tell us of His miracles and His ministry; His sayings and His doings; His life and His death; His power and His love; His kindness and His patience; His ways, His words, His works, His thoughts, His heart. Blessed be God, there is one thing in the Bible the most prejudiced reader can hardly fail to understand, and that is the character of Jesus Christ!

How encouraging are the examples the Bible gives us of good people! It tells us of many who were of like passions with ourselves—men and women who had cares, crosses, families, temptations, afflictions, diseases, like ourselves—and yet "by faith and patience inherited the promises," and got safe home (Hebrews 6:12). It keeps back nothing in the history of these people. Their mistakes, their infirmities, their conflicts, their experience, their prayers, their praises, their useful lives, their happy deaths—all are fully recorded. And it tells us the God and Saviour of these men and women still waits to be gracious, and is altogether unchanged.

How instructive are the examples the Bible gives us of bad people! It tells us of men and women who had light, and knowledge, and opportunities, like ourselves, and yet hardened their hearts, loved the world, clung to their sins, would have their own way, despised reproof, and ruined their own souls forever. And it warns that the God who punished Pharaoh, and Saul, and Ahab, and Jezebel, and Judas, and Ananias and Sapphira, is a God who never alters, and that there is a hell.

How precious are the promises which the Bible contains for the use of those who love God! There is hardly any possible emergency or condition for which it has not some "word in season."[1] And it tells men that God loves to be put in remembrance of these promises, and that if He has said He will do a thing, His promise shall certainly be performed.

How blessed are the hopes which the Bible holds out to the believer in Christ Jesus! Peace in the hour of death, rest and happiness on the other side of the grave, a glorious body in the morning of the resurrection, a full and triumphant acquittal in

---

[1] Isaiah 50:4.

the day of judgment, an everlasting reward in the kingdom of Christ, a joyful meeting with the Lord's people in the day of gathering together—these, these are the future prospects of every true Christian. They are all written in the book—in the book which is all true.

How striking is the light which the Bible throws on the character of man! It teaches us what men may be expected to be and do in every position and station of life. It gives us the deepest insight into the secret springs and motives of human actions, and the ordinary course of events under the control of human agents. It is the true "discerner of the thoughts and intents of the heart" (Hebrews 4:12). How deep is the wisdom contained in the books of Proverbs and Ecclesiastes! I can well understand an old divine saying, "Give me a candle and a Bible, and shut me up in a dark dungeon, and I will tell you all that the whole world is doing."

Reader, all these are things which men could find nowhere except in the Bible. We have probably not the least idea how little we should know about these things if we had not the Bible. We hardly know the value of the air we breathe, and the sun which shines on us, because we have never known what it is to be without them. We do not value the truths on which I have been just now dwelling, because we do not realize the darkness of men to whom these truths have not been revealed. Surely no tongue can fully tell the value of the treasures this one volume contains. Well might old John Newton say that some books were *copper* books in his estimation, some were *silver*, and some few were *gold*—but the Bible alone was like a book all made up of *bank notes*.[1]

Think not for a moment that any part of this precious book is not profitable. Think not that such portions as catalogues and pedigrees, as Leviticus and the description of Ezekiel's temple,

---

[1] Before his salvation, John Newton (1725–1807) was an utterly corrupt slave-trading profligate, given over to the basest sins; afterwards, however, he was ordained to the Anglican ministry and will always be remembered for composing "Amazing Grace," a glorious hymn with the heartfelt line, "that saved a wretch like me."

are useless and without value. Believe me it is childish folly to question the usefulness of any word in the Bible merely because our eyes at present do not see its use.

Come with me, and look for a moment at the book of nature, and I will soon show you things of which you do not see the use.

Place yourself in imagination by the side of an Australian gold-digging, and observe the earth that is drawn up from its bottom. It is likely that your unpractised eyes will see nothing in that heap but rubbish, and dirt, and stones. And yet that very heap of earth may prove, on washing, to be full of particles of the purest gold. It is just the same with the Bible. We see but a little of it now. We shall find hereafter that every verse of it contained gold.

Place yourself in imagination on the top of some Highland mountain. Look at the minute moss or lichen which clings to the side of that mass of rock. Tell me, if you can, what use and purpose that lichen serves. The birds of the air, the beasts of the field, the very insects, leave it alone. The grouse, the ptarmigan, and red deer draw no sustenance from it. The rock does not require its covering. And yet that minute lichen is as truly a part of God's creation as the cedars of Lebanon, or the *Victoria regia* of the South American rivers. Place it under a microscope, and you will soon see that like all other works of God, it is "very good,"[1] and full of beautiful design. Settle it down in your mind that as it is with the book of nature, so it is with the book of revelation, the written Word of God. There is not a chapter or verse from first to last which is not in some way profitable. If you and I do not see its use, it is because we have not eyes to see it yet. But all, we may rest assured, is precious. All is "very good." Well said Bishop Jewell, "There is no sentence, no clause, no word, no syllable, no letter, but it is written for thy instruction. There is not one jot but it is signed and sealed with the blood of the Lamb."[2]

[1] Genesis 1:31.

[2] John Jewell (1522–1571), Bishop of Salisbury, was a theologian whose works clarified the doctrinal distinctions between Anglicanism and Catholicism, during the reign of Queen Elizabeth.

Reader, this is the Book about which I address you this day. Surely it is no light matter *what you are doing with it*. It is no light matter in what way you are using this treasure. I charge you, I summon you to give an honest answer to my question—What art thou doing with the Bible? Dost thou read it? How READEST THOU?

IV. I ask, in the fourth place, because *no book in existence has produced such wonderful effects on mankind at large as the Bible.*

(*a*) This is the Book whose doctrines turned the world upside down in the days of the apostles.

Eighteen centuries have now passed away since God sent forth a few Jews from a remote corner of the earth to do a work which, according to man's judgment, must have seemed impossible. He sent them forth at a time when the whole world was full of superstition, cruelty, lust, and sin. He sent them forth to proclaim that the established religions of the earth were false and useless, and must be forsaken. He sent them forth to persuade men to give up old habits and customs, and to live different lives. He sent them forth to do battle with vested interests, and old associations, with a bigoted priesthood, with sneering philosophers, with an ignorant population, with bloody-minded emperors, with the whole influence of Rome. Never was there an enterprise to all appearance more Quixotic,[1] and less likely to succeed!

And how did He arm them for this battle? He gave them no carnal weapons. He gave them no worldly power to compel assent, and no worldly riches to bribe belief. He simply put the Holy Ghost into their hearts, and the Scriptures into their hands. He simply bade them to expound and explain, to enforce and to publish the doctrines of the Bible. The preacher of Christianity in the first century was not a man with a sword and an army, to frighten people, like Mahomet, or a man with a license to be sensual, to allure people, like the priests of the shameful

---

[1] Idealistic without regard to practicality; caught up in the romance of noble deeds and the pursuit of unreachable goals.

idols of Hindostan. No! he was nothing more than one holy man with one holy book.

And how did these men of one book prosper? In a few generations they entirely changed the face of society by the doctrines of the Bible. They emptied the temples of the heathen gods. They famished idolatry, or left it high and dry like a stranded ship. They brought into the world a higher tone of morality between man and man. They raised the character and position of woman. They altered the standard of purity and decency. They put an end to many cruel and bloody customs, such as the gladiatorial fights. There was no stopping the change. Persecution and opposition were useless. One victory after another was won. One bad thing after another melted away. Whether men liked it or not, they were insensibly affected by the movement of the new religion, and drawn within the whirlpool of its power. The earth shook, and their rotten refuges fell to the ground. The flood rose, and they found themselves obliged to rise with it. The tree of Christianity swelled and grew, and the chains they had cast round it to arrest its growth snapped like tow. And all this was done by the doctrines of the Bible! Talk of victories indeed! What are the victories of Alexander, and Cæsar, and Marlborough, and Napoleon, and Wellington compared with those I have just mentioned? For extent, for completeness, for results, for permanence, there are no victories like the victories of the Bible.

(b) This is the Book which turned Europe upside down in the days of the glorious Protestant Reformation.

No man can read the history of Christendom as it was five hundred years ago and not see that darkness covered the whole professing church of Christ, even a darkness that might be felt. So great was the change that had come over Christianity that if an apostle had risen from the dead, he would not have recognised it, and would have thought that heathenism had revived again. The doctrines of the Bible lay buried under a dense mass of human traditions. Penances, and pilgrimages, and indulgences, relic-worship, and image-worship, and saint-worship, and worship of the Virgin Mary, formed the sum and substance of most people's religion. The Church was made an idol. The priests and ministers of the Church usurped the place of Christ. And by what means was all this miserable darkness cleared away? By none so much as by bringing forth once more the Bible.

It was not merely the preaching of Luther and his friends which established Protestantism in Germany. The grand lever which overthrew the Pope's power in that country was Luther's translation of the Bible into the German tongue. It was not merely the writings of Cranmer and the English Reformers which cast down Popery in England. The seeds of the work thus carried forward were first sown by Wycliffe's translation of the Bible many years before. It was not merely the quarrel of Henry VIII and the Pope of Rome which loosened the Pope's hold on English minds. It was the royal permission to have the Bible translated and set up in churches, so that everyone who liked might read it. Yes! it was the reading and circulation of Scripture which mainly established the cause of Protestantism in England, in Germany, and Switzerland. Without it the people would probably have returned to their former bondage when the first Reformers died. But by reading of the Bible the public mind became gradually leavened with the principles of true religion. Men's eyes became thoroughly open. Their spiritual understandings became thoroughly enlarged. The abominations of Popery became distinctly visible. The excellence of the pure gospel became a rooted idea in their hearts. It was then in vain for popes to thunder forth excommunications. It was useless for kings and queens to attempt to stop the course of Protestantism by fire and sword. It was all too late. The people knew too much. They had seen the light. They had heard the joyful sound. They had tasted the truth. The sun had risen on their minds. The scales had fallen from their eyes. The Bible had done its appointed work within them, and that work was not to be overthrown. The people would not return to Egypt. The clock could not be put back again. A mental and moral revolution had been effected, and mainly effected by God's Word. Oh! reader, those are the true revolutions which the Bible effects. What are all the revolutions recorded by Vertot[1]—what are all the revolutions which France and England have gone through, compared to these? No revolutions are so bloodless, none so satisfactory, none so rich in lasting results, as the revolutions accomplished by the Bible!

This is the Book on which the well-being of nations has always hinged, and with which the best interests of every nation in Christendom at this moment are inseparably bound up. It is a great fact that the Bible has had a most extraordinary effect on the condition of those nations in which it has been known, taught, and read. Just in proportion as the Bible is honoured or not, light or darkness, morality or immorality, true religion or superstition, liberty or despotism, good laws or bad, will be found in a land. Come with me and open the pages of history, and you will read the proofs in time past. Read it in the history of Israel under the Kings. How great was the wickedness that then prevailed! But who can wonder? The law of the Lord had been completely lost sight of, and was found in the days of Josiah thrown aside in a corner of the temple (2 Kings 22:8). Read it in the history of the Jews in our Lord Jesus Christ's time. How awful the picture of scribes and Pharisees, and their religion! But who can wonder? The Scripture was "made of none effect by man's traditions" (Matthew 15:6). Read it in the history of the Church of Christ in the Middle Ages. What can be worse than the accounts we have of their ignorance and superstition? But who can wonder? The times might well be dark when men had not the light of the Bible.

Come with me next and look at the map of the world, and see what a tale it tells! Which are the countries where the greatest amount of ignorance, superstition, immorality, and tyranny are to be found at this very moment? The countries in which the Bible is a forbidden or neglected book—such countries as Italy, and Spain, and the South American states. Which are the countries where liberty, and public and private morality, have

---

[1] René Aubert de Vertot (1655–1735), French historian whose specialty was political revolutions.

attained the highest pitch? The countries where the Bible is free to all, like England, Scotland, and the United States. Yes! when you know how a nation deals with the Bible, you may generally know what a nation is. Oh! that the rulers of some nations did but know that a free Bible is the grand secret of national prosperity, and that the surest way to make subjects orderly and obedient is to allow a free passage to the living waters of God's Word! Oh! that the people of some countries did but see that a free Bible is the beginning of all real freedom, and that the first liberty they should seek after is liberty for the apostles and prophets—liberty to have a Bible in every house, and a Bible in every hand! Well said Bishop Hooper, "God in heaven and the king on earth have no greater friend than the Bible."[1] It is a striking fact that when British sovereigns are crowned, they are publicly presented with the Bible, and told, "This book is the most valuable thing this world affords."

This is the Book which at this moment is producing the mightiest moral and spiritual effects throughout the world. This is the secret of the wonderful success which attends the London City Mission and the Irish Church Missions. This is the true account of that amazing move towards Protestantism which has lately taken place in several departments of France. Which are the cities of the earth where the fewest soldiers and police are required to keep order? London, Manchester, Liverpool, New York—cities which are deluged with Bibles. Which are the churches on earth which are producing the greatest effect on mankind? The churches in which the Bible is exalted. Which are the parishes in England and Scotland where religion and morality have the strongest hold? The parishes in which the Bible is most circulated and read. Who are the ministers in England who have the most real influence over the minds of the people? Not those who are ever crying "Church! Church!" but those who are faithfully preaching the Word. Ah! reader, a church which does not honour the Bible is as useless as a body without life, or a

[1] John Hooper (1495–1555), Bishop of Gloucester and martyr: J.C. Ryle profiles his life and ministry, including his horrifying death at the stake, in *Light From Old Times.*

steam engine without fire. A minister who does not honour the Bible is as useless as a soldier without arms, a builder without tools, a pilot without compass, or a messenger without tidings. It is cheap and easy work for Roman Catholics, neologians, and friends of secular education to sneer at those who love the Bible. But the Romanist, the neologian, and the friends of mere secular education have never yet shewn us one New Zealand, one Tinnevelly, one Sierra Leone as the fruit of their principles.[1] We only can do that who honour the Bible, and we say these are the works of the Word, and the proofs of its power.

This is the Book to which the civilized world is indebted for many of its best and most praiseworthy institutions. Few probably are aware how many are the good things that men have adopted for the public benefit, of which the origin may be clearly traced up to the Bible. It has left lasting marks wherever it has been received. From the Bible are drawn many of the best laws by which society is kept in order. From the Bible has been obtained the standard of morality about truth, honesty, and the relations of man and wife, which prevails among Christian nations, and which, however feebly respected in many cases, makes so great a difference between Christians and heathen. To the Bible we are indebted for that most merciful provision for the poor man, the Sabbath day. To the influence of the Bible we owe nearly every humane and charitable institution in existence. The sick, the poor, the aged, the orphan, the lunatic, the idiot, the blind, were seldom or never thought of before the Bible leavened the world. You may search in vain for any record of institutions for their aid in the histories of Athens or Rome. Ah! reader, many sneer at the Bible, and say the world would get on well enough without it, who little think how great are their own obligations to the Bible. Little does the infidel think, as he lies sick in one of our great hospitals, that he owes all his present comforts to the very book he affects to despise. Had it not been

---

[1] Three remote missionary colonies founded by evangelicals: New Zealand in the South Pacific, Tinnevelly in southeastern India, and Sierra Leone in western Africa.

for the Bible, he might have died in misery, uncared for, unnoticed, and alone. Verily the world we live in is fearfully unconscious of its debts. The last day alone, I believe, will tell the full amount of benefit conferred upon it by the Bible.

Reader, this wonderful book is the subject about which I address you this day. Surely it is no light matter *what you are doing with the Bible*. The swords of conquering generals, the ship in which Nelson led the fleets of England to victory, the hydraulic press which raised the tubular bridge at the Menai—each and all of these are objects of interest as instruments of mighty power.[1] The book I speak of this day is an instrument a thousandfold mightier still. Surely it is no light matter whether you are paying it the attention it deserves. I charge you, I summon you to give me an honest answer this day—What art thou doing with the Bible? Dost thou read it? How readest thou?

V. I ask, in the fifth place, because *no book in existence can do so much for everyone who reads it rightly as the Bible.*

The Bible does not profess to teach the wisdom of this world. It was not written to explain geology or astronomy. It will neither instruct you in mathematics nor in natural philosophy. It will not make you a doctor, or a lawyer, or an engineer.

But there is another world to be thought of beside that world in which man now lives. There are other ends for which man was created besides making money and working. There are other interests which he is meant to attend to besides those of his body—and those interests are the interests of his soul.

The interests of the immortal soul are the interests which the Bible is especially able to promote. If you would know law, you

[1] The HMS *Victory*, an exceptional 100-gun ship of the line, was Admiral Horatio Nelson's (1758–1805) flagship in the Battle of Trafalgar, where twenty French and Spanish ships were destroyed, while not one single British vessel was lost.

The Britannia Bridge (built 1846–49) is a tubular railroad bridge, spanning Menai Strait (Wales), made of two completely enclosed wrought-iron tubes, which were joined in the middle. Capstan and hydraulic power lifted the rectangular tubes into place, each weighing about 1500 tons.

may study Blackstone or Sugden. If you would know astronomy or geology, you may study Herschel and Lyell. But if you would know how to have your soul saved, you must study the written Word of God.

Reader, the Bible is *"able to make a man wise unto salvation, through faith which is in Christ Jesus"* (2 Timothy 3:15). It can show you the way which leads to heaven. It can teach you everything you need to know, point out everything you need to believe, and explain everything you need to do. It can show you what you are—*a sinner*. It can show you what God is—perfectly *holy*. It can show you the great giver of pardon, peace, and grace—*Jesus Christ*. I have read of an Englishman who visited Scotland in the days of Blair, Rutherford, and Dickson—three famous preachers—and heard all three in succession. He said that the first showed him the majesty of God, the second showed him the beauty of Christ, and the third showed him all his heart. It is the glory and beauty of the Bible that it is always teaching these three things, more or less, from the first chapter of it to the last.

The Bible applied to the heart by the Holy Ghost is *the grand instrument by which souls are first converted to God*. That mighty change is generally begun by some text or doctrine of the Word brought home to a man's conscience. In this way the Bible has worked moral miracles by thousands. It has made drunkards become sober, unchaste people become pure, thieves become honest, and violent-tempered people become meek. It has wholly altered the course of men's lives. It has caused their old things to pass away, and made all their ways new. It has taught worldly people to seek first the kingdom of God. It has taught lovers of pleasure to become lovers of God. It has taught the stream of men's affections to run upwards instead of running downwards. It has made them think of heaven, instead of always thinking of earth, and live by faith, instead of living by sight. All this it has done in every part of the world. All this it is doing still. What are the pretended Romish miracles, which weak men believe, compared to all this, even if they were true? Those are the truly great miracles which are yearly worked by the Word.

The Bible applied to the heart by the Holy Ghost is *the chief means by which men are built up and established in the faith*, after their conversion. It is able to cleanse them, to sanctify them, to instruct them in righteousness, and to furnish them thoroughly for all good works (Psalm 119:9; John 17:17; 2 Timothy 3:16, 17). The Spirit ordinarily does these things by the written Word, sometimes by the Word read, and sometimes by the Word preached; but seldom, if ever, without the Word. The Bible can show a believer how to walk in this world so as to please God. It can teach him how to glorify Christ in all the relations of life, and can make him a good master, servant, subject, husband, father, or son. It can enable him to bear afflictions and privations without murmuring, and say, "It is well" (2 Kings 4:23, 26). It can enable him to look down into the grave, and say, "I fear no evil" (Psalm 23:4). It can enable him to think on judgment and eternity, and not feel afraid. It can enable him to bear persecution without flinching, and to give up liberty and life rather than deny Christ's truth. Is he drowsy in soul? It can awaken him. Is he mourning? It can comfort him. Is he erring? It can restore him. Is he weak? It can make him strong. Is he in company? It can keep him from evil. Is he alone? It can talk with him (Proverbs 6:22). All this the Bible can do for all believers—for the least as well as the greatest, for the richest as well as the poorest. It has done it for thousands already, and is doing it for thousands every day.

Reader, the man who has the Bible has everything which is absolutely needful to make him spiritually wise. He needs no priest to break the bread of life for him. He needs no ancient traditions, no writings of the Fathers, no voice of the Church, to guide him into all truth. He has the well of truth open before him, and what can he want more? Yes! though he be shut up alone in a prison, or cast on a desert island—though he never see a church, or minister, or sacrament again—if he has but the Bible, he has got the infallible guide, and wants no other. If he has but the will to read that Bible rightly, it shall certainly teach him the road that leads to heaven. It is here alone that infallibility resides. It is not in the Church. It is not in the councils. It is not in ministers. It is only in the written Word.

(*a*) I know well that many say they have found no saving power in the Bible. They tell us they have tried to read it and have learned nothing from it. They can see in it nothing but hard and deep things. They ask us what we mean by talking of its power.

I answer that the Bible no doubt contains hard things, or else it would not be the Book of God. It contains things hard to comprehend, but only hard because we have not grasp of mind to comprehend them. It contains things above our reasoning powers, but nothing that might not be explained if the eyes of our understanding were not feeble and dim. But is not an acknowledgment of our own ignorance the very cornerstone and foundation of all knowledge? Must not many things be taken for granted in the beginning of every science before we can proceed one step towards acquaintance with it? Do we not require our children to learn many things of which they cannot see the meaning at first? And ought we not then to expect to find "deep things"[1] when we begin studying the Word of God, and yet to believe that if we persevere in reading it, the meaning of many of them will one day be made clear? No doubt we ought so to expect, and so to believe. We must read with humility. We must take much on trust. We must believe that what we know not now, we shall know hereafter, some part in this world, and all in the world to come.

But I ask that man who has given up reading the Bible, because it contains hard things, whether he did not find many things in it easy and plain. I put it to his conscience, whether he did not see great landmarks and leading principles in it all the way through. I ask him whether the things needful to salvation did not stand out boldly before his eyes, like the lighthouses on English headlands from the Land's End to the mouth of the Thames. What should we think of the captain of a steamer who brought up at night in the entrance of the Channel on the plea that he did not know every parish, and village, and creek, along the British coast? Should we not think him a lazy coward, when

[1] Job 12:22; 1 Corinthians 2:10.

the lights on the Lizard, and Eddystone, and the Start, and Port-land, and St. Catherine's, and Beachy Head, and Dungeness, and the Forelands were shining forth like so many lamps to guide him up to the river? Should we not say, "Why did you not steer by the great leading lights?" And what ought we to say to the man who gives up reading the Bible, because it contains hard things, when his own state, and the path to heaven, and the way to serve God are all written down clearly and unmistakably, as with a sunbeam? Surely we ought to tell that man that his objections are no better than lazy excuses, and do not deserve to be heard.

(b) I know well that many raise the objection that thousands read the Bible, and are not a whit the better for their reading. And they ask us, when this is the case, what becomes of the Bible's boasted power.

I answer that the reason why so many read the Bible without benefit is plain and simple—they do not read it in the right way. There is generally a right way and a wrong way of doing everything in the world; and just as it is with other things, so it is in the matter of reading the Bible. The Bible is not so entirely different from all other books as to make it of no importance in what spirit and manner you read it. It does not do good, as a matter of course, by merely running our eyes over the print, any more than the sacraments do good by mere virtue of our receiving them. It does not ordinarily do good, unless it is read with humility and earnest prayer. The best steam-engine that was ever built is useless if a man does not know how to work it. The best sundial that was ever constructed will not tell its owner the time of day, if he is so ignorant as to put it up in the shade. Just as it is with that steam engine, and that sundial, so it is with the Bible. When men read it without profit, *the fault is not in the Book, but in themselves.*

I tell the man who doubts the power of the Bible, because many read and are no better for the reading, that the abuse of a thing is no argument against the use of it. I tell him boldly that never did man or woman read that book in a childlike persevering spirit—like the Ethiopian eunuch, and the Bereans—and miss the way to heaven (Acts 8:28; 17:11). Yes! many a broken cistern will be exposed to shame in the day of judgment, but there will not rise up one soul who will be able to say that he went thirsting to the Bible and found in it no living water; he searched for truth in the Scriptures, and searching, did not find it. The words which are spoken of Wisdom in the Proverbs are strictly true of the Bible:

> If thou criest after knowledge, and liftest up thy voice for understanding; If thou seekest her as silver, and searchest for her as for hid treasures; Then shalt thou understand the fear of the LORD, and find the knowledge of God. (Proverbs 2:3–5)

Reader, this wonderful book is the subject about which I address you this day. Surely it is no light matter *what you are doing with the Bible*. What should you think of the man who, in time of cholera, despised a sure receipt for preserving the health of his body? What must be thought of you, if you despise the only sure receipt for the everlasting health of your soul? I charge you, I entreat you, to give an honest answer to my question. What dost thou do with the Bible? Dost thou read it? How READEST THOU?

VI. I ask, in the sixth place, because *no gift of God to man is so awfully neglected and misused as the Bible.*

Man has an unhappy skill in abusing God's gifts. His privileges, and power, and faculties are all ingeniously perverted to other ends than those for which they were bestowed. His speech, his imagination, his intellect, his strength, his time, his influence, his money—instead of being used as instruments for glorifying his Maker—are generally employed for his own selfish ends. And just as man naturally makes a bad use of his other mercies, so he does of the written Word. One sweeping charge may be brought against the whole of Christendom, and that charge is neglect and abuse of the Bible.

Reader, I know that this charge sounds awful. Listen to me, and I will give you proofs to substantiate it. Awful as it is, it is sadly true.

It is true of the Roman Catholic Church, from one end of the world to the other. For six hundred years that unhappy church has waged open war with the Bible, and has laboured incessantly to prevent people reading it. By a rule deliberately passed in the great Council of Trent,[1] by the bulls of Popes, by the encyclical letters of Romish bishops, by the repeated open hostility of Romish priests—the views of the Church of Rome on this subject have been made fully manifest. Of all the numerous and soul-ruining errors of which the Church of Rome is guilty, none is more mischievous and productive of evil than its treatment of the Bible.

It is truly fearful to consider how thoroughly at variance God and the Church of Rome are about the Bible. The Lord God has declared positively that Holy Scripture is "profitable," that it is "given for our learning," that it is "able to make men wise unto salvation," that it is "the sword" which a soldier of Christ should be armed with, that it is "a light to our feet," and that all errors arise from ignorance of it.[2] The Church of Rome, on the other hand, has declared positively, in the Council of Trent, that "If the Holy Scriptures be everywhere allowed indiscriminately in the vulgar tongue, more harm than good will arise from it," and that "If any one shall presume to read, or possess, a Bible, without license, he shall not receive absolution, except he first deliver it up." A license to read the Bible! What a blasphemous insult is this! It would sound as well to talk of a license to breathe God's air, or look at God's sun. Well may the Church of Rome be in gross darkness, when it pours such contempt on the written Word.

It is useless to assert, as some do, that statements such as these are not correct. It is useless to tell us that Bibles are openly paraded for sale in Roman Catholic shop windows in English towns. The Church of Rome dares not yet show itself in its true colours in England. It winks at practices contrary to its avowed

---

[1] The Council of Trent (1545–63) is the single most important event in the history of the Roman Catholic Church; to this day Rome has not repudiated any of its decrees.

[2] 2 Timothy 3:16; Romans 15:4; 2 Tim. 3:15; Ephesians 6:17; Psalm 119:105.

principles because it suits its purpose to do so. It throws dust in the eyes of simple people, by the appearance of toleration; and so blinds them to its real character. But the Church of Rome at heart is always the same.

Ask anyone who has lived in countries on the Continent, where the power of the Pope is unrestrained, and see what he will tell you. Ask anyone, especially, who has lived in Italy, and been at Rome, and seen Roman Catholic religion in full bloom, and mark what kind of account he will give you. If a man would know what real pure Presbyterianism is, he must go to Scotland. If he would know what real pure Church-of-Englandism is, he must visit England. If he would know what real, pure, genuine Romanism is, he should go to Italy and Rome.

Is it not a fact that to have or read an Italian Bible is one of the highest crimes an Italian can commit? He may commit adultery and fornication—he may stab, or lie, or rob, or swear, or cheat —and get absolution from his priest without much difficulty. But woe be to the Italian who dares to have or read God's holy Word! That fact speaks volumes. Let that fact be thoroughly known all over the world.

Is it not a fact that the Bible itself cannot be bought at Rome, unless with immense difficulty, and at an immense price? You may buy books of many other kinds and descriptions—worthless French novels, frivolous Italian poetry, miserable lying accounts of pretended miracles done by pretended saints, prayers to the Virgin Mary, and all manner of literary rubbish. You may buy poisons, daggers, or intoxicating drinks. You may buy relics, and rosaries, and scapulars, and crucifixes. You may buy masses and services to redeem your father's soul from purgatory. But one thing it is almost impossible to buy, and that is the one book needful—the written Word of God. You may easily buy all means and appliances for doing the works of darkness. You cannot buy the grand help for doing the works of light, except at an enormous cost. That fact alone speaks volumes. Oh! that the world would awake and know it! THE BIBLE IS PRACTICALLY A FORBIDDEN BOOK AT ROME.

Ah! reader, it is an awful thought that all these insults to the

Bible are perpetrated in the name of Christianity! It is an awful thought that a day of reckoning is yet to come, and that God, the Judge of all, is just as jealous about His *word*, as about His *name* and *day!* It is an awful thought that even the Emperor of China will rise up in judgment with the Pope, and condemn him; for he has lately decreed that the New Testament is a profitable book, and may be read. It is an awful thought that this Bible-proscribing Church of Rome contains more members than any other church in the world! Surely I have a right to say, no gift from God is so neglected and misused as the Bible.

But the Church of Rome, unhappily, is not the only professedly Christian church whose members are guilty in this matter. The charge of neglecting the Bible is one which may be brought home to the members of Protestant churches also, and among others to the Protestants of England and Scotland in the present day.

I write this statement down with sorrow. I dare say it will be received by some with surprise, if not with incredulity. But I write it down calmly and deliberately, and I am certain it is true.

I am well aware that there are more Bibles in Great Britain at this moment than there ever were since the world began. There is more Bible buying and Bible selling, more Bible printing and Bible distributing, than ever was since England was a nation. We see Bibles in every bookseller's shop—Bibles of every size, price, and style—Bibles great, and Bibles small—Bibles for the rich, and Bibles for the poor. But all this time I fear we are in danger of forgetting that to *have* the Bible is one thing, and to *read* it quite another.

I am firmly persuaded that the Bible of many a man and woman in Great Britain is *never read at all.* In one house it lies in a corner, stiff, cold, glossy, and fresh as it was when it came from the bookseller's shop. In another it lies on a table, with its owner's name written in it—a silent witness against him day after day. In another it lies on some high shelf, neglected and dusty, to be brought down only on grand occasions, such as a birth in the family, like a heathen idol at its yearly festival. In another it lies deep down at the bottom of some box or drawer, among the things not wanted, and is never dragged forth into the light of day, until the arrival of sickness, the doctor, and death. Ah! these things are sad and solemn. But they are true.

I am firmly persuaded that many in Great Britain who read the Bible *do not read it aright.* One man looks over a chapter on Sunday evening—but that is all. Another reads a chapter every day to his servants at family prayers—but that is all. A third goes a step further and hastily reads a verse or two in private every morning, before he goes out of his house. A fourth goes further still and reads as much as a chapter or two every day, though he does it in a great hurry, and omits it on the smallest pretext. But each and every one of these men does what he does in a heartless, scrambling, formal kind of way. He does it coldly as a duty. He does not do it with appetite and pleasure. He is glad when the task is over. He forgets it all when the book is shut. Oh! what a sad picture is this! But in multitudes of cases, oh! how true.

But how do I know all this? What makes me speak so confidently? Listen to me a few moments and I will lay before you some evidence. Neglect of the Bible is like disease of the body. It shows itself in the face of a man's conduct. It tells it own tale. It cannot be hid.

I am sure that many neglect the Bible, *because of the enormous ignorance of true religion which everywhere prevails.* There are thousands of professing Christians in this Protestant country who know literally nothing about the gospel. They could not give you the slightest account of its distinctive doctrines. They have no more idea of the meaning of conversion, grace, faith, justification, and sanctification than of so many words and names in Arabic. If you were to ask them whether regeneration, and the new creature, were a beast, a man, or a doctrine, they could not tell. And can I suppose such persons read the Scriptures? I cannot suppose it. I do not believe they do.

I am sure that many neglect the Bible, *because of the utter indifference with which they regard false doctrine.* They will talk with perfect coolness of others having become Roman Catholics, or Socinians, or Mormonites, as if it were all the same thing in the long run. And can I suppose such persons search the Scriptures? I cannot suppose it. I do not believe they do.

I am sure that many neglect the Bible, *because of the readiness with which they receive false doctrines.* They are led astray by the first preacher of lies they meet with, who has a pleasant voice, a nice manner, and a gift of eloquent speech. They swallow all he says without enquiry, and believe him as implicitly as Papists do the Pope. And can I suppose such persons search the Scriptures? I cannot suppose it. I do not believe they do.

I am sure that many neglect the Bible, *because of the bitterness with which they contend for some little secondary unimportant point in religion.* They make a "Shibboleth"[1] of their own little cherished point, and are ready to set down every one as "no Christian," if he does not see it with their eyes. And can I suppose such persons really search the whole Scriptures? I cannot suppose it. I do not believe they do.

I am sure that many neglect the Bible, *because of the very scanty knowledge they have of its contents.* They know a certain set of doctrines. They can repeat a certain string of hackneyed texts. But they never seem to get beyond this little string. Let a man talk to them about some text out of their beaten path, and he is at once out of their depth. They listen, but have nothing to say. Let a minister preach to them anything but the merest elements of Christianity, and they appear shocked at him as a rash and unsound teacher. In short, they seem content to remain in the condition described by St. Paul to the Hebrews: always unskilful in the word of righteousness—always in a state of religious babyhood. And can I suppose such persons really search the Scriptures? I cannot suppose it. I do not believe they do.

I am sure that many neglect the Bible, *because of the lives they live.* They do the very things that God plainly forbids. They neglect the very things that God plainly commands. They break God's laws week after week without shame. And can I suppose such persons search the Scriptures? I allow that much knowledge of the Bible and much wickedness of heart may sometimes

[1] Judges 12:6.

be found together. But when I see a wicked life, I generally believe there is a neglected Bible.

I am sure that many neglect the Bible, *because of the deaths they die*. They send for a minister in their last moments, and ask for the "consolations of religion." And in what state are they found? They know nothing whatever of the way of salvation. They have to be told which are the first principles of the gospel of Christ. And can I suppose such persons have searched the Scriptures? I cannot suppose it. I do not believe they have.

I bring forward all this evidence with sorrow. I know well it will be offensive to some. But I believe I have stated nothing but glaring facts, which every true Christian and true minister of Christ's gospel will readily confirm. And I say that these facts prove the existence of a sore evil in Great Britain—I mean a neglected Bible. These things would never be, if the Bible was thoroughly *read* by many, as well as *possessed*.

Ah! reader, it is a painful thought that there should be so much profession of love to the Bible among us, and so little proof that the Bible is read! Here we are, as a nation, pluming ourselves on our Protestantism, and yet neglecting the foundation on which Protestantism is built! Here we are, thanking God with our lips, like the Pharisee, that we are not Papists, as some are, and yet dishonouring God's Word! It is an awful thought that the people of this country will be judged according to their light, and that so many of them should be keeping that light under a bushel! Truly I have cause for saying, no gift of God is so neglected as the Bible.

Reader, this neglected book is the subject about which I address you this day. Surely it is no light matter *what you are doing with the Bible*. Surely when the plague is abroad, you should search and see whether the plague-spot is on you. I charge you, I entreat you, to give an honest answer to my question. What art thou doing with the Bible? Dost thou read it? How READEST THOU?

VII. I ask, in the seventh place, because *the Bible is the only rule by which all questions of doctrine or of duty can be tried.*

The Lord God knows the weakness and infirmity of our poor fallen understandings. He knows that, even after conversion, our perceptions of right and wrong are exceedingly indistinct. He knows how artfully Satan can gild error with an appearance of truth, and can dress up wrong with plausible arguments, till it looks like right. Knowing all this, He has mercifully provided us with an unerring standard of truth and error, right and wrong, and has taken care to make that standard a written book—even the Scripture.

No one can look round the world, and not see the wisdom of such a provision. No one can live long, and not find out that he is constantly in need of a counsellor and adviser—of a rule of faith and practice, on which he can depend. Unless he lives like a beast, without a soul and conscience, he will find himself constantly assailed by difficult and puzzling questions. He will be often asking himself, What must I believe? and what must I do?

(*a*) The world is full of difficulties about points of *doctrine*. The house of error lies close alongside the house of truth. The door of one is so like the door of the other that there is continual risk of mistakes.

Does a man read or travel much? He will soon find the most opposite opinions prevailing among those who are called Christians. He will discover that different persons give the most different answers to the important question, "What shall I do to be saved?"[1] The Roman Catholic and the Protestant, the neologian and the Tractarian, the Mormonite and the Swedenborgian—each and all will assert that he alone has the truth. Each and all will tell him that safety is only to be found in his party. Each and all say, "Come with us."[2] All this is puzzling. What shall a man do?

Does he settle down quietly in some English or Scotch parish? He will soon find that even in our own land the most conflicting views are held. He will soon discover that there are serious dif-

---

[1] Acts 16:30.   [2] Proverbs 1:11.

ferences among Christians, as to the comparative importance of the various parts and articles of the faith. One man thinks of nothing but church government; another of nothing but sacraments, services, and forms; a third of nothing but preaching the gospel. Does he apply to ministers for a solution? He will perhaps find one minister teaching one doctrine, and another another. Does he go to the bishops for help? He will find what one bishop says is right, another says is wrong. All this is puzzling. What shall a man do?

There is only one answer to this question. A man must make the Bible alone his rule. He must receive nothing, and believe nothing, which is not according to the Word. He must try all religious teaching by one simple test—Does it square with the Bible? What saith the Scripture?

I would to God the eyes of the laity of this country were more open on this subject. I would to God they would learn to weigh sermons, books, opinions, and ministers, in the scales of the Bible, and to value all according to their conformity to the Word. I would to God they would see that it matters little who says a thing—whether he be Father or Reformer, bishop or archbishop, priest or deacon, archdeacon or dean. The only question is—Is the thing said scriptural? If it is, it ought to be received and believed. If it is not, it ought to be refused and cast aside. I fear the consequences of that servile acceptance of everything which the "parson says," which is so common among many English laymen. I fear lest they be led they know not whither, like the blinded Syrians, and awake some day to find themselves in the power of Rome (2 Kings 6:20). Oh! that men in England would only remember for what purpose the Bible was given them!

I tell English laymen that it is nonsense to say, as some do, that it is presumptuous to judge a minister's teaching by the Word. When one doctrine is proclaimed in one parish, and another in another, people must read and judge for themselves. Both doctrines cannot be right, and both ought to be tried by the Word. I charge them, above all things, never to suppose that any true minister of the gospel will dislike his people measuring all he teaches by the Bible. On the contrary, the more they read the Bible, and prove all he says by the Bible, the better he will be pleased. A false minister may say, "You have no right to use your private judgment: leave the Bible to us who are ordained." A true minister will say, "Search the Scriptures, and if I do not teach you what is scriptural, do not believe me." A false minister may cry, "Hear the Church," and "Hear me." A true minister will say, "Hear the Word of God."[1]

(b) But the world is not only full of difficulties about points of doctrine. It is equally full of difficulties about points of *practice*. Every professing Christian, who wishes to act conscientiously, must know that it is so. The most puzzling questions are continually arising. He is tried on every side by doubts as to the line of duty, and can often hardly see what is the right thing to do.

He is tried by questions connected with the management of his *worldly calling*, if he is in business or in trade. He sometimes sees things going on of a very doubtful character—things that can hardly be called fair, straightforward, truthful, and doing as you would be done by. But then everybody in the trade does these things. They have always been done in the most respectable houses. There would be no carrying on a profitable business if they were not done. They are not things distinctly named and prohibited by God. All this is very puzzling. What is a man to do?

He is tried by questions of a *political kind*, if he occupies a high position in life. He finds that men do things in their public capacity which they would not think of doing in their private one. He finds that men are expected to sacrifice their own judgment, private opinion, and conscience, to the interests of their own party, and to believe that the acts of their own political friends are always right, and the acts of their political opponents always wrong. All this is puzzling. What is a man to do?

He is tried by questions in the matter of *speaking truth*. He hears things said continually which he knows are not correct. He hears a false colouring put on stories, which he knows ought

[1] Luke 11:28.

to wear a different aspect. He sees additions to, and subtractions from, the whole truth. He sees evasions, and equivocations, and concealments of facts in every class of society, when self-interests are at stake. He hears false compliments paid, and false excuses alleged, and false characters given. But then it is the way of the world. Everybody does so. Nobody means any harm by it. All this is very puzzling. What is he to do?

He is tried by questions about *sabbath observance*. Can there really be any harm in travelling, or writing letters, or keeping accounts, or reading newspapers on Sunday? Is it wrong to take a situation on a railway, merely because the Sunday traffic would almost entirely keep him away from public worship? Would it be wrong to open the Crystal Palace at Sydenham on Sundays? Is not Christianity a religion of liberty? Do not many learned, and respectable, and titled people think that Sunday should be a day for recreation? All this is very puzzling. What is a man to do?

He is tried by questions about *worldly amusements*. Races, and balls, and operas, and theatres, and card parties are all very doubtful methods of spending time. But he sees numbers of great people taking part in them. Are all these people wrong? Can there really be such mighty harm in these things? All this is very puzzling. What is a man to do?

He is tried by questions about the *education of his children*. He wishes to train them up morally and religiously, and to remember their souls. But he is told by many sensible people that young persons will be young, that it does not do to check and restrain them too much, and that he ought to attend pantomimes and children's parties, and give children's balls himself. He is informed that this nobleman, or that lady of rank, always does so, and yet they are reckoned religious people. Surely it cannot be wrong. All this is very puzzling. What is he to do?

He is tried by questions about *reading*. He does not wish to read what is really bad, and has not time for much reading beside the Bible. Ought he, or ought he not, to read such things as sceptical writings, or French novels, or semi-popish poetry? Can there really be much harm in it? Do not many persons, as good as himself, read these things? And after all, the Bible has not expressly forbidden Emerson or Eugéne Sue. All this is very puzzling. What is he to do?

There is only one answer to all these questions. A man must make the Bible his rule of conduct. He must make its leading principles the compass by which he steers his course through life. By the letter or spirit of the Bible he must test every difficult point and question. *"To the law, and to the testimony! What saith the Scripture?"*[1] He ought to care nothing for what other people may think right. He ought not to set his watch by the clock of his neighbour, but by the sundial of the Word.

Reader, I charge you solemnly to act on the maxim I have just laid down, and to adhere to it rigidly all the days of your life. You will never repent of it. Make it a leading principle never to act contrary to the Word. Care not for the charge of overstrictness and needless precision. Remember, you serve a strict and holy God. Listen not to the common objection that the rule you have laid down is impossible, and cannot be observed in such a world as this. Let those who make such an objection speak out plainly, and tell us for what purpose the Bible was given to man. Let them remember that by the Bible we shall all be judged at the last day, and let them learn to judge themselves by it here, lest they be judged and condemned by it hereafter.

Reader, this mighty rule of faith and practice is the Book about which I am addressing you this day. Surely it is no light matter *what you are doing with the Bible.* Surely when danger is abroad on the right hand and on the left, you should consider what you are doing with the safeguard which God has provided. I charge you, I beseech you, to give an honest answer to my question. What art thou doing with the Bible? Dost thou read it? HOW READEST THOU?

VIII. I ask, in the next place, because *the Bible is the book which all true servants of God have always lived on and loved.*

Every living thing which God creates requires food. The life that God imparts needs sustaining and nourishing. It is so with

---

[1] Isaiah 8:20; Romans 4:3; Galatians 4:30.

animal and vegetable life—with birds, beasts, fishes, reptiles, insects, and plants. It is equally so with spiritual life. When the Holy Ghost raises a man from the death of sin, and makes him a new creature in Christ Jesus, the new principle in that man's heart requires food, and the only food which will sustain it is the Word of God.

There never was a man or woman truly converted, from one end of the world to the other, who did not love the revealed will of God. Just as a child born into the world desires naturally the milk provided for its nourishment, so does a soul "born again"[1] desire the sincere milk of the Word. This is a common mark of all the children of God—they "delight in the law of the Lord" (Psalm 1:2).

Show me a person who despises Bible reading, or thinks little of Bible preaching, and I hold it to be a certain fact that he is not yet "born again." He may be zealous about forms and ceremonies. He may be diligent in attending sacraments and daily services. But if these things are more precious to him than the Bible, I cannot think he is a converted man. Tell me what the Bible is to a man, and I will generally tell you what he is. This is the pulse to try—this is the barometer to look at—if we would know the state of the heart. I have no notion of the Spirit dwelling in a man and not giving clear evidence of His presence. And I believe it to be a signal evidence of the Spirit's presence when the Word is really precious to a man's soul.

Love to the Word is one of the characteristics we see in Job. Little as we know of this patriarch and his age, this at least stands out clearly. He says, "I have esteemed the words of His mouth more than my necessary food" (Job 23:12).

Love to the Word is a shining feature in the character of David. Mark how it appears all through that wonderful part of Scripture, the One hundred nineteenth Psalm. He might well say, "O how love I Thy law"! (Psalm 119:97.)

Love to the Word is a striking point in the character of St. Paul. What were he and his companions but men "mighty in the

---

[1] John 3:3, 7; 1 Peter 1:23.

Scriptures"?[1] What were his sermons but expositions and applications of the Word?

Love to the Word appears preëminently in our Lord and Saviour Jesus Christ. He read it publicly. He quoted it continually. He expounded it frequently. He advised the Jews to "search" it.[2] He used it as His weapon to resist the devil. He said repeatedly, "The Scripture must be fulfilled."[3] Almost the last thing He did was to "open the understanding of His disciples, that they might understand the Scriptures" (Luke 24:45). Ah! reader, that man can be no true servant of Christ, who has not something of his Master's mind and feeling toward the Bible.

Love to the Word has been a prominent feature in the history of all the saints, of whom we know anything, since the days of the apostles. This is the lamp which Athanasius, and Chrysostom, and Augustine followed. This is the compass which kept the Vallenses from making shipwreck of the faith. This is the well which was reopened by Wycliffe and Luther, after it had been long stopped up. This is the sword with which Latimer, and Jewell, and Knox won their victories. This is the manna which fed Baxter, and Owen, and the noble host of the Puritans, and made them strong to battle. This is the armoury from which Whitefield and Wesley drew their powerful weapons. This is the mine from which Bickersteth and M'Cheyne brought forth rich gold.[4] Differing as these holy men did in some matters, on one point they were all agreed—they all delighted in the Word.

[1] Acts 18:24.   [2] John 5:39.   [3] Mark 14:49.

[4] All of these names are a representative sweep through Church history. Athanasius (c. 293–373), Chrysostom (c. 354–407), and Augustine (354–430) are known as "church fathers"; the Vallenses were French proto-Protestants from the Middle Ages; John Wycliffe (c. 1330–1384) was the first man to translate the entire Bible into English; Martin Luther (1483–1546) was the German theologian who initiated the Reformation; Hugh Latimer (1485–1555), John Jewell (1522–1571), and John Knox (c. 1514–1572) were instrumental in shaping the English/Scotch Reformations; Richard Baxter (1615–1691) and John Owen (1616–1683) were two leaders of Puritanism, a movement committed to the purity & reformation of the Church; George Whitefield (1714–1770) and John Wesley (1703–1791) were brilliant preachers during the Great Awakening; and Edward Bickersteth (1786–1850) and Robert M'Cheyne (1813–1843) were faithful ministers of the gospel, whose lives bring the survey to the period when Ryle first published this paper (1852).

Love to the Word is one of the first things that appears in the converted heathen, at the various missionary stations throughout the world. In hot climates and in cold, among savage people and among civilized, in New Zealand, in the South Sea Islands, in Africa, in Hindostan—it is always the same. They enjoy hearing it read. They long to be able to read it themselves. They wonder why Christians did not send it to them before. How striking is the picture which Moffat draws of Africaner, the fierce South African chieftain, when first brought under the power of the gospel! "Often have I seen him," he says, "under the shadow of a great rock nearly the livelong day, eagerly perusing the pages of the Bible." How touching is the expression of a poor converted negro, speaking of the Bible! He said, "It is never old and never cold." How affecting was the language of another old negro, when some would have dissuaded him from learning to read, because of his great age. "No!" he said, "I will never give it up till I die. It is worth all the labour to be able to read that one verse, 'God so loved the world, that He gave His only begotten Son, that whosoever believeth in Him should not perish, but have eternal life.'" (John 3:16.)

Love to the Bible is one of the grand points of agreement among all converted men and women in our land. Episcopalians and Presbyterians, Baptists and Independents, Methodists and Plymouth Brethren—all unite in honouring the Bible, as soon as they are real Christians. This is the manna which all the tribes of our Israel feed upon, and find satisfying food. This is the fountain round which all the various portions of Christ's flock meet together, and from which no sheep goes thirsty away. Oh! that believers in this country would learn to cleave more closely to the written Word! Oh! that they would see that the more the Bible, and the Bible only, is the substance of man's religion, the more they agree! It is probable there never was an uninspired book more universally admired than Bunyan's *Pilgrim's Progress*.[1]

---

[1] John Bunyan (1628–1688) was a self-taught preacher of the gospel, who spent twelve years in jail, being persecuted for his faith. During his imprisonment he wrote the spiritual classic *Pilgrim's Progress*, a wonderful allegorical tale of the Christian walk.

It is a book which all denominations of Christians delight to honour. It has won praise from all parties. Now what a striking fact it is that the author was preëminently a man of one book! He had read hardly anything but the Bible.

Away with the foolish idea that making the Bible alone the rule of faith hinders unity, and that those who profess to glory in the Bible, and nothing but the Bible, are hopelessly divided! It is a weak invention of the enemy. It is a base calumny. No doubt there is much dissension and party spirit among mere outward professors; but among the great bulk of believing Protestants there is a wonderful amount of unity—real, thorough, and deep, far deeper than the boasted unity of Rome. Their differences are merely about the outward trappings of Christianity. About the body of the faith they are all agreed. Their differences are studiously exaggerated by the enemies of true religion. Their points of agreement—such as the *Harmony of Protestant Confessions* exhibits—are studiously kept out of sight. Their differences are differences which in times of common danger are soon forgotten. Their unity is an unity which in front of sin, heathenism, and persecution, stands boldly out. Ridley and Hooper forgot their old disagreements when they found themselves in Queen Mary's prisons. Churchmen and Nonconformists laid aside their quarrels when James II tried to bring back Popery to England. Protestant missionaries, of different denominations, find they can work and pray together, when they are in the midst of idolaters. Protestant believers in London have proved to the world that they can agree to labour together for the conversion of souls, maintaining that glorious institution, the London City Mission. And what is the secret of all this deep-seated unity? It comes from this—That all believers on earth are not only born of one Spirit, but also read one holy book, and feed on the bread of one Bible.

Ah! reader, it is a blessed thought that there will be "much people" in heaven at last. Few as the Lord's people undoubtedly are at any given time or place, yet all gathered together at last, they will be "a multitude that no man can number." (Revelation 19:1; 7:9.) They will be of one heart and mind. They will have passed through like experience. They will all have repented, believed, lived holy, prayerful, and humble. They will all have washed their robes and made them white in the blood of the Lamb. But one thing beside all this they will have in common. They will all love the texts and doctrines of the Bible. The Bible will have been their food and delight, in the days of their pilgrimage on earth. And the Bible will be a common subject of joyful meditation and retrospect, when they are gathered together in heaven.

Reader, this book, which all true Christians live upon and love, is the subject about which I am addressing you this day. Surely it is no light matter *what you are doing with the Bible.* Surely it is matter for serious inquiry, whether you know anything of this love to the Word, and have this mark of "walking in the footsteps of the flock" (Song of Solomon 1:8). I charge you, I entreat you, to give me an honest answer. What art thou doing with the Bible? Dost thou read it? How READEST THOU?

IX. I ask, in the last place, because *the Bible is the only book which can comfort a man in the last hours of his life.*

Death is an event which in all probability is before us all. There is no avoiding it. It is the river which each of us must cross. I who write, and you who read, have each one day to die. It is good to remember this. We are all sadly apt to put away the subject from us. "Each man thinks each man mortal but himself."[1] I want every one to do his duty in life, but I also want every one to think of death. I want everyone to know how to live, but I also want everyone to know how to die.

Death is a solemn event to all. It is the winding up of all earthly plans and expectations. It is a separation from all we have loved and lived with. It is often accompanied by much bodily pain and distress. It brings us to the grave, the worm, and corruption. It opens the door to judgment and eternity—to heaven or to hell. It is an event after which there is no change, or space

---

[1] Edward Young (1683–1765), *The Complaint: or Night Thoughts on Life, Death, and Immortality.*

for repentance. Other mistakes may be corrected or retrieved, but not a mistake on our deathbeds. As the tree falls, there it must lie. No conversion in the coffin! No new birth after we have ceased to breathe! And death is before us all. It may be close at hand. The time of our departure is quite uncertain. But sooner or later we must each lie down alone and die. All these are serious considerations.

Death is a solemn event, even to the believer in Christ. For him no doubt the "sting of death" is taken away (1 Corinthians 15:55). Death has become one of his privileges, for he is Christ's. Living or dying, he is the Lord's. If he lives, Christ lives in him; and if he dies, he goes to live with Christ. To him "to live is Christ, and to die is gain" (Philippians 1:21). Death frees him from many trials—from a weak body, a corrupt heart, a tempting devil, and an ensnaring or persecuting world. Death admits him to the enjoyment of many blessings. He rests from his labours—the hope of a joyful resurrection is changed into a certainty; he has the company of holy redeemed spirits—he is "with Christ."[1] All this is true; and yet, even to a believer, death is a solemn thing. Flesh and blood naturally shrink from it. To part from all we love is a wrench and trial to the feelings. The world we go to is a world unknown, even though it is our home. Friendly and harmless as death is to a believer, it is not an event to be treated lightly. It always must be a very solemn thing.

Reader, it becomes every one to consider calmly how he is going to meet death. Gird up your loins, like a man, and look the subject in the face. Listen to me while I tell you a few things about the end to which we are coming.

The good things of the world cannot comfort a man when he draws near death. All the gold of California and Australia will not provide light for the dark valley. Money can buy the best medical advice and attendance for a man's body. But money cannot buy peace for his conscience, heart, and soul.

Relatives, loved friends, and servants cannot comfort a man when he draws near death. They may minister affectionately to

[1] Philippians 1:23.

his bodily wants. They may watch by his bedside tenderly, and anticipate his every wish. They may smooth down his dying pillow, and support his sinking frame in their arms. But they cannot "minister to a mind diseased."[1] They cannot stop the achings of a troubled heart. They cannot screen an uneasy conscience from the eye of God.

The pleasures of the world cannot comfort a man when he draws near death. The brilliant ballroom, the merry dance, the midnight revel, the party to Epsom races, the card table, the box at the opera, the voices of singing men and singing women—all these are at length distasteful things. To hear of hunting and shooting engagements gives him no pleasure. To be invited to feasts, and regattas, and fancy fairs gives him no ease. He cannot hide from himself that these are hollow, empty, powerless things. They jar upon the ear of his conscience. They are out of harmony with his condition. They cannot stop one gap in his heart, when the last enemy is coming in like a flood. They cannot make him calm in the prospect of meeting a holy God.

Books and newspapers cannot comfort a man when he draws near death. The most brilliant writings of Macaulay or Dickens will pall upon his ear. The most able article in the *Times* will fail to interest him. The *Edinburgh* and *Quarterly* reviews will give him no pleasure. *Punch* and the *Illustrated News*, and the last new novel, will lie unopened and unheeded. Their time will be past. Their vocation will be gone. Whatever they may be in health, they are useless in the hour of death.

There is but one fountain of comfort for a man drawing near to his end, and that is the Bible. Chapters out of the Bible, texts out of the Bible, statements of truth taken out of the Bible, books containing matter drawn from the Bible—these are a man's only chance of comfort when he comes to die. I do not at all say that the Bible will do good, as a matter of course, to a dying man, if he has not valued it before. I know, unhappily, too much of deathbeds to say that. I do not say whether it is probable that he who has been unbelieving and neglectful of the Bible in life will at once believe and get comfort from it in death. But

---

[1] *Macbeth*, V, III, 40, by William Shakespeare (1564–1616).

I do say positively that no dying man will ever get real comfort, except from the contents of the Word of God. All comfort from any other source is a house built upon sand.

I lay this down as a rule of universal application. I make no exception in favour of any class on earth. Kings and poor men, learned and unlearned—all are on a level in this matter. There is not a jot of real consolation for any dying man, unless he gets it from the Bible. Chapters, passages, texts, promises, and doctrines of Scripture—heard, received, believed, and rested on—these are the only comforters I dare promise to any one, when he leaves the world. Taking the sacrament will do a man no more good than the Popish extreme unction, so long as the Word is not received and believed. Priestly absolution will no more ease the conscience than the incantations of a heathen magician, if the poor dying sinner does not receive and believe Bible truth. I tell everyone who reads this paper that, although men may seem to get on comfortably without the Bible while they live, they may be sure that without the Bible they cannot comfortably die. It was a true confession of the learned Selden, "There is no book upon which we can rest in a dying moment but the Bible."[1]

I might easily confirm all I have just said by examples and illustrations. I might show you the deathbeds of men who have affected to despise the Bible. I might tell you how Voltaire and Paine—the famous infidels—died in misery, bitterness, rage, fear, and despair.[2] I might show you the happy deathbeds of

[1] John Selden (1584–1654) was an exceptional scholar and the leading lay-member of the Westminster Assembly. Near the end of his life his soul found rest in Titus 2:11–15.

[2] Voltaire (1694–1778), Frenchman, writer, philosopher, and reprobate, was as wretched in death as he was in life. Upon his deathbed he cried out, "I am abandoned by God and man! I will give you half of what I am worth if you will give me six months' life. Then I shall go to hell; and you will go with me. O Christ! O Jesus Christ!" The nurse who attended him said, "For all the wealth in Europe I would not see another infidel die."

Anglo-American writer Thomas Paine (1737–1809) fared little better than the Frenchman on his deathbed. He said, "O Lord, help me! Christ, help me! O God, what have I done to suffer so much? But there is no God! But if there should be, what will become of me hereafter? Stay with me, for God's sake! Send even a child to stay with me, for it is hell to be alone. If ever the devil had an agent, I have been that one."

those who have loved the Bible and believed it, and the blessed effect the sight of their deathbeds had on others. Cecil—a minister whose praise ought to be in all churches—says, "I shall never forget standing by the bedside of my dying mother. 'Are you afraid to die?' I asked. 'No!' she replied. 'But why does the uncertainty of another state give you no concern?' 'Because God has said, "Fear not; when thou passest through the waters I will be with thee, and through the rivers, they shall not overflow thee."'" (Isaiah 43:2.) I might easily multiply illustrations of this kind. But I think it better to conclude this part of my subject by giving the result of my own observations as a minister.

I have seen not a few dying persons in my time. I have seen great varieties of manner and deportment among them. I have seen some die sullen, silent, and comfortless. I have seen others die ignorant, unconcerned, and apparently without much fear. I have seen some die so wearied with long illness that they were quite willing to depart, and yet they did not seem to me at all in a fit state to go before God. I have seen others die with professions of hope and trust in God, without leaving satisfactory evidences that they were on the rock. I have seen others die who, I believe, were "in Christ"[1] and safe, and yet they never seemed to enjoy much sensible comfort. I have seen some few dying in the full assurance of hope, and like Bunyan's "Standfast," giving glorious testimony to Christ's faithfulness, even in the river. But one thing I have never seen. I never saw any one enjoy what I should call real, solid, calm, reasonable peace on his deathbed, who did not draw his peace from the Bible. And this I am bold to say, that the man who thinks to go to his deathbed without having the Bible for his comforter, his companion, and his friend, is one of the greatest madmen in the world. There are no comforts for the soul but Bible comforts, and he who has not got hold of these, has got hold of nothing at all, unless it be a broken reed.

Reader, the only comforter for a deathbed is the Book about which I address you this day. Surely it is no light matter whether

[1] Romans 8:1; 2 Corinthians 5:17.

you read that book or not. Surely a dying man, in a dying world, should seriously consider whether he has got anything to comfort him, when his turn comes to die. I charge you, I entreat you, for the last time, to give an honest answer to my question. What art thou doing with the Bible? Dost thou read it? How READEST THOU?

Reader, I have now given you the reasons why I ask you a question about the Bible on the present occasion. I have shown you that knowledge of the Bible is absolutely necessary to salvation; that no book is written in such a manner as the Bible; that no book contains such matter; that no book has done so much for the world generally; that no book can do so much for everyone who reads it aright; that no book is so awfully neglected; that this book is the only rule of faith and practice; that it is, and always has been, the food of all true servants of God; and that it is the only book which can comfort men when they die. All these are ancient things. I do not pretend to tell you anything new. I have only gathered together old truths, and tried to mould them into a new shape. Let me finish all, by addressing a few plain words to the conscience of every class of readers.

(1) These pages may fall into the hands of some who can read, but never do read the Bible at all. Reader, are you one of them? If you are, I have something to say to you.

I cannot comfort you in your present state of mind. It would be mockery and deceit to do so. I cannot speak to you of peace and heaven, while you treat the Bible as you do. You are in danger of losing your soul.

You are in danger, because *your neglected Bible is a plain evidence that you do not love God.* The health of a man's body may generally be known by his appetite. The health of a man's soul may be known by his treatment of the Bible. Now you are manifestly labouring under a sore disease. Reader, will you not repent?

You are in danger, because *God will reckon with you for your neglect of the Bible in the day of judgment.* You will have to give account of your use of time, strength, and money; and you will also have to give account of your use of the Word. You will not stand at that bar side by side with the Patagonian, who never heard of the Bible. Oh, no! To whom much is given, of them much will be required. Of all men's buried talents, none will weigh them down so heavily as a neglected Bible. As you deal with the Bible, so God will deal with your soul. Reader, I say again, will you not repent, and turn over a new leaf in life, and read your Bible?

You are in danger, because *there is no degree of error in religion into which you may not fall.* You are at the mercy of the first clever Jesuit, Mormonite, Socinian, Turk, or Jew, who may happen to meet you. A land of unwalled villages is not more defenceless against an enemy than the man who neglects his Bible. You may go on tumbling from one step of delusion to another, till at length you are landed in the pit of hell. Reader, I say once more, will you not repent and read your Bible?

You are in danger, because *there is not a single reasonable excuse you can allege for neglecting the Bible.* You have no time to read it forsooth! But you can make time for eating, drinking, sleeping, and perhaps for newspaper reading and smoking. You might easily make time to read the Word. Alas! it is not want of time, but waste of time that ruins souls. You find it too troublesome to read forsooth! You had better say at once it is too much trouble to go to heaven, and you are content to go to hell. Truly these excuses are like the rubbish round the walls of Jerusalem in Nehemiah's days. They would all soon disappear if, like the Jews, you had "a mind to work."[1] Reader, I say for the last time, will you not repent and read your Bible?

I know I cannot reach your heart. I cannot make you see and feel these things. I can only enter my solemn protest against your present treatment of the Bible, and lay that protest before your conscience. I do so with all my soul. Oh! beware lest you repent too late! Beware lest you put off seeking for the Bible till you send for the doctor in your last illness, and then find the Bible a sealed book, and dark as the cloud between the hosts of Israel and Egypt, to your anxious soul! Beware lest you go on saying all

[1] Nehemiah 4:6.

your life, "Men do very well without all this Bible-reading," and find at length, to your cost, that men do very ill, and end in hell! Beware lest the day come, when you will feel, "Had I but honoured the Bible as much as I have honoured the newspaper, I should not have been left without comfort in my last hour!" Bible-neglecting reader, I give you a plain warning. The plague-cross is at present on your door. The Lord have mercy upon your soul![1]

(2) These pages may fall into the hands of someone who is willing to begin reading the Bible, but wants advice on the subject. Reader, are you that man? Listen to me, and I will give you a few short hints.

(a) For one thing, *begin reading your Bible this very day*. The way to do a thing is to do it, and the way to read the Bible is actually to read it. It is not meaning, or wishing, or resolving, or intending, or thinking about it, which will advance you one step. You must positively read. There is no royal road in this matter, any more than in the matter of prayer. If you cannot read yourself, you must persuade somebody else to read to you. But one way or another, through eyes or ears, the words of Scripture must actually pass before your mind.

(b) For another thing, *read the Bible with an earnest desire to understand it*. Think not for a moment that the great object is to turn over a certain quantity of printed paper, and that it matters nothing whether you understand it or not. Some ignorant people seem to fancy that all is done if they clear off so many chapters every day, though they may not have a notion what they are all about, and only know that they have pushed on their mark so many leaves. This is turning Bible-reading into a mere form. It is almost as bad as the Popish habit of buying indulgences by saying an almost fabulous number of *Ave Marias* and Paternosters. It reminds one of the poor Hottentot who ate up a Dutch hymn-book because he saw it comforted his neighbours' hearts. Settle

---

[1] During the Great Plague of London (1665), infected victims were boarded up in their homes; the door was then marked with a red cross and the words "Lord have mercy on us" were inscribed on it. Death was imminent, usually within four days.

it down in your mind, as a general principle, that a Bible not understood is a Bible that does no good. Say to yourself often as you read, "What is all this about?" Dig for the meaning like a man digging for Australian gold. Work hard, and do not give up the work in a hurry.

(c) For another thing, *read the Bible with deep reverence.* Say to your soul, whenever you open the Bible, "O my soul, thou art going to read a message from God." The sentences of judges and the speeches of kings are received with awe and respect. How much more reverence is due to the words of the Judge of judges and King of kings! Avoid, as you would cursing and swearing, that irreverent habit of mind, into which some modern divines have unhappily fallen, in speaking about the Bible. They handle the contents of the holy book as carelessly and disrespectfully as if the writers were such men as themselves. They make one think of a child composing a book to expose the fancied ignorance of his own father, or of a pardoned murderer criticising the handwriting and style of his own reprieve, or of a man botanising on his mother's grave. Enter rather into the spirit of the words spoken to Moses on Mount Horeb: "Put thy shoes from off thy feet; the place whereon thou standest is holy ground."[1]

(d) For another thing, *read the Bible with earnest prayer for the teaching and help of the Holy Spirit.* Here is the rock on which many make shipwreck at the very outset. They do not ask for wisdom and instruction, and so they find the Bible dark, and carry nothing away from it. You should pray for the Spirit to guide you into all truth. You should beg the Lord Jesus Christ to "open your understanding,"[2] as He did that of His disciples. The Lord God, by whose inspiration the Book was written, keeps the keys of the Book, and alone can enable you to understand it profitably. Nine times over in one psalm does David cry, "Teach me." Five times over in the same psalm does he say, "Give me understanding."[3] Well says John Owen, Dean of Christ Church, Oxford, "There is a sacred light in the Word: but there is a covering and veil on the eyes of men, so that they cannot behold it

---

[1] Exodus 3:5.   [2] Luke 24:45.   [3] Psalm 119.

J.C. RYLE

aright. Now the removal of this veil is the peculiar work of the Holy Spirit." Humble prayer will throw more light on your Bible than Poole's *Synopsis*, or all the commentaries that were ever written. Remember this, and say always, "O God, for Christ's sake, give me the teaching of the Spirit."

(*e*) For another thing, *read the Bible with childlike faith and humility*. Open your heart as you open your book, and say, "Speak, LORD, for Thy servant heareth."[1] Resolve to believe implicitly whatever you find there, however much it may run counter to your own prejudices. Resolve to receive heartily every statement of truth, whether you like it or not. Beware of that miserable habit of mind into which some readers of the Bible fall. They receive some doctrines, because they like them. They reject others, because they are condemning to themselves, or to some lover, or relation, or friend. At this rate the Bible is useless. Are we to be judges of what ought to be in the Word? Do we know better than God? Settle it down in your mind that you will receive all, and believe all, and that what you cannot understand you will take on trust. Remember, when you pray, you are speaking to God, and God hears you. But, remember, when you read, God is speaking to you, and you are not to "answer again,"[2] but to listen.

(*f*) For another thing, *read the Bible in a spirit of obedience and self-application*. Sit down to the study of it with a daily determination that *you* will live by its rules, rest on its statements, and act on its commands. Consider, as you travel through every chapter, "How does this affect *my* position and course of conduct? What does this teach *me*?" It is poor work to read the Bible for mere curiosity and speculative purposes, in order to fill your head and store your mind with opinions, while you do not allow the book to influence your heart and life. That Bible is read best, which is practised most.

(*g*) For another thing, *read the Bible daily*. Make it a part of every day's business to read and meditate on some portion of God's Word. Private means of grace are just as needful every day

[1] 1 Samuel 3:9, 10.   [2] Luke 14:6.

for our souls, as food and clothing are for our bodies. Yesterday's bread will not feed the labourer today, and today's bread will not feed the labourer tomorrow. Do as the Israelites did in the wilderness. Gather your manna fresh every morning. Choose your own seasons and hours. Do not scramble over and hurry your reading. Give your Bible the best, and not the worst, part of your time. But whatever plan you pursue, let it be a rule of your life to visit the throne of grace and the Bible every day.

(h) For another thing, *read all the Bible, and read it in an orderly way.* I fear there are many parts of the Word which some people never read at all. This is, to say the least, a very presumptuous habit. "All Scripture is profitable" (2 Timothy 3:16). To this habit may be traced the want of broad, well-proportioned views of truth, which is so common in this day. Some people's Bible-reading is a system of perpetual dipping and picking. They do not seem to have an idea of regularly going through the whole book. This also is a great mistake. No doubt in times of sickness and affliction it is allowable to search out seasonable portions. But with this exception, I believe it is by far the best plan to begin the Old and New Testaments at the same time, read each straight through to the end, and then begin again. This is a matter in which every one must be persuaded in his own mind. I can only say it has been my own plan for forty years, and I have never seen cause to alter it.

(i) For another thing, *read the Bible fairly and honestly.* Determine to take everything in its plain, obvious meaning, and regard all forced interpretations with great suspicion. As a general rule, whatever a verse of the Bible seems to mean, it does mean. Cecil's rule is a very valuable one—"The right way of interpreting Scripture is to take it as we find it, without any attempt to force it into any particular system." Well said Hooker, "I hold it for a most infallible rule in the exposition of Scripture that when a literal construction will stand, the furthest from the literal is commonly the worst."

(j) In the last place, *read the Bible with Christ continually in view.* The grand primary object of all Scripture is to testify of Jesus. Old Testament ceremonies are shadows of Christ. Old Testament judges and deliverers are types of Christ. Old Testament history shows the world's need of Christ. Old Testament prophecies are full of Christ's sufferings, and of Christ's glory yet to come. The first advent and the second, the Lord's humiliation and the Lord's kingdom, the cross and the crown, shine forth everywhere in the Bible. Keep fast hold on this clue, if you would read the Bible aright.

Reader, I might easily add to these hints, if time permitted. Few and short as they are, you will find them worth attention. Act upon them, and I firmly believe you will never be allowed to miss the way to heaven. Act upon them, and you will find light continually increasing in your mind. No book of evidence can be compared with that internal evidence which he obtains, who daily uses the Word in the right way. Such a man does not need the books of learned men, like Paley, and Wilson, and M'Ilvaine.[1] He has the witness in himself. The Book satisfies and feeds his soul. A poor Christian woman once said to an infidel, "I am no scholar. I cannot argue like you. But I know that honey is honey, because it leaves a sweet taste in my mouth. And I know the Bible to be God's book, because of the taste it leaves in my heart."

(3) These pages may fall into the hands of someone who *loves and believes the Bible, and yet reads it but little.* I fear there are many such in this day. It is a day of bustle and hurry. It is a day of talking, and committee meetings, and public work. These things are all very well in their way, but I fear that sometimes they clip and cut short the private reading of the Bible. Reader, does your conscience tell you that you are one of the persons I speak of? Listen to me, and I will say a few things which deserve your serious attention.

You are the man that is likely to *get little comfort from the Bible in time of need.* Trial is a sifting season. Affliction is a searching wind, which strips the leaves off the trees, and brings to light the birds' nests. Now I fear that your stores of Bible consolations

---

[1] William Paley (1743–1805), Daniel Wilson (1778–1858), and Charles M'Ilvaine (1799–1873) were theologians who wrote on the subject of evidences for the Christian faith.

may one day run very low. I fear lest you should find yourself at last on very short allowance, and come into harbour weak, worn, and thin.

You are the man that is likely *never to be established in the truth*. I shall not be surprised to hear that you are troubled with doubts and questionings about assurance, grace, faith, perseverance, and the like. The devil is an old and cunning enemy. Like the Benjamites, he can "throw stones at a hair breadth, and not miss" (Judges 20:16). He can quote Scripture readily enough, when he pleases. Now you are not sufficiently ready with your weapons to be able to fight a good fight with him. Your armour does not fit you well. Your sword sits loosely in your hand.

You are the man that is likely to *make mistakes in life*. I shall not wonder if I am told that you have erred about your own marriage, erred about your children's education, erred about the conduct of your household, erred about the company you keep. The world you steer through is full of rocks, and shoals, and sandbanks. You are not sufficiently familiar either with the lights or charts.

You are the man that is likely to *be carried away by some specious false teacher for a season*. It will not surprise me if I hear that some one of those clever, eloquent men, who can "make the worse appear the better cause,"[1] is leading you into many follies. You are wanting in ballast. No wonder if you are tossed to and fro, like a cork on the waves.

Reader, all these are uncomfortable things. I want you to escape them all. Take the advice I offer you this day. Do not merely read your Bible "a little," but read it a great deal. "Let the word of Christ dwell in you richly" (Colossians 3:16). Do not be a mere babe in spiritual knowledge. Seek to become "well-instructed in the kingdom of heaven,"[2] and to be continually adding new things to old. A religion of feeling is an uncertain thing. It is like the tide, sometimes high, and sometimes low. It is like the moon, sometimes bright, and sometimes dim. A religion of deep Bible-knowledge is a firm and lasting possession. It

---

[1] *Paradise Lost,* by John Milton (1608–1674).   [2] Matthew 13:52.

enables a man not merely to say, "I feel hope in Christ," but "I know whom I have believed" (2 Timothy 1:12).

(4) These pages may fall into the hands of someone who *reads the Bible much, and yet fancies he is no better for his reading.* This is a crafty temptation of the devil. At one stage he says, "Do not read the Bible at all." At another he says, "Your reading does you no good: give it up." Reader, are you that man? I feel for you from the bottom of my soul. Let me try to do you good.

Do not think you are getting no good from the Bible, merely because you do not see that good day by day. The greatest effects are by no means those which make the most noise, and are most easily observed. The greatest effects are often silent, quiet, and hard to detect at the time they are being produced. Think of the influence of the moon upon the earth, and of the air upon the human lungs. Remember how silently the dew falls, and how imperceptibly the grass grows. There may be far more doing than you think in your soul by your Bible-reading.

The Word may be gradually producing deep *impressions* on your heart, of which you are not at present aware. Often when the memory is retaining no facts, the character of a man is receiving some everlasting impression. Is sin becoming every year more hateful to you? Is Christ becoming every year more precious? Is holiness becoming every year more lovely and desirable in your eyes? If these things are so, take courage. The Bible is doing you good, though you may not be able to trace it out day by day.

The Bible may be restraining you from some sin or delusion, into which you would otherwise run. It may be daily keeping you back, and hedging you up, and preventing many a false step. Ah! reader, you might soon find this out to your cost, if you were to cease reading the Word. The very familiarity of blessings sometimes makes us insensible to their value. Resist the devil. Settle it down in your mind as an established rule that, whether you feel it at the moment or not, you are inhaling spiritual health by reading the Bible, and insensibly becoming more strong.

(5) There may be some into whose hands these pages will fall who *really love the Bible, live upon the Bible, and read it much.*

Reader, are you one of these? Give me your attention, and I will mention a few things which we shall do well to lay to heart for time to come.

Let us resolve to *read the Bible more and more* every year we live. Let us try to get it rooted in our memories, and engrafted into our hearts. Let us be thoroughly well provisioned with it against the voyage of death. Who knows but we may have a very stormy passage? Sight and hearing may fail us, and we may be in deep waters. Oh, to have the Word "hid in our hearts" in such an hour as that! (Psalm 119:11.)

Let us resolve to be *more watchful over our Bible-reading* every year that we live. Let us be jealously careful about the time we give to it, and the manner that time is spent. Let us beware of omitting our daily reading without sufficient cause. Let us not be gaping, and yawning, and dozing over our book while we read. Let us read like a London merchant studying the City article in the *Times*, or like a wife reading a husband's letter from a distant land. Let us be very careful that we never exalt any minister, or sermon, or book, or tract, or friend, above the Word. Cursed be that book, or tract, or human counsel which creeps in between us and the Bible, and hides the Bible from our eyes! Once more I say, let us be very watchful. The moment we open the Bible, the devil sits down by our side to tempt us. Oh! to read with a hungry spirit, and a simple desire for edification!

Let us resolve to *honour the Bible more in our families*. Let us read it morning and evening to our children and households, and not be ashamed to let men see that we do so. Let us not be discouraged by seeing no good arise from it. The Bible-reading in a family has kept many a one from the gaol, the workhouse, and the *Gazette*, if it has not kept him from hell.

Let us resolve to *meditate more on the Bible*. It is good to take with us two or three texts, when we go out into the world, and to turn them over in our minds, whenever we have a little leisure. It keeps out many vain thoughts. It clenches the nail of daily reading. It preserves our souls from stagnating, and breeding corrupt things. It sanctifies and quickens our memories, and prevents their becoming like those ponds where the frogs live, but the fish die.

Let us resolve to *talk more to believers about the Bible* when we meet them. Alas! the conversation of Christians, when they do meet, is often sadly unprofitable. How many frivolous, and trifling, and uncharitable things are said! Let us bring out the Bible more, and it will help to drive the devil away, and keep our hearts in tune. Oh! that we may all strive so to walk together in this evil world that Jesus may often draw near and go with us, as He went with the two disciples journeying to Emmaus!

Let us resolve to *prize the Bible more*. Let us not fear being idolaters of this blessed book. Men may easily make an idol of the Church, of ministers, of sacraments, or of intellect. Men cannot make an idol of the Word. Let us regard all who would damage the authority of the Bible, or impugn its credit, as spiritual robbers. We are travelling through a wilderness: they rob us of our only guide. We are voyaging over a stormy sea: they rob us of our only compass. We are toiling over a weary road: they pluck our staff out of our hands. And what do these spiritual robbers give us in place of the Bible? What do they offer as a guide and provision for our souls? Nothing! absolutely nothing! Big swelling words! Empty promises of new light! High sounding jargon, but nothing substantial and real. They would fain take from us the bread of life, and they do not give us in its place so much as a stone. Let us turn a deaf ear to them. Let us firmly grasp and prize the Bible more and more, the more it is assaulted.

Let us resolve to *remember those who have not got the Bible*. Let us labour to raise them from their low estate. None are so poor as those who have not the Scriptures. Let us think of them with pity and compassion, and not judge them by the standard of people who have the Word.

Let us deal gently with our Irish brother. He may do many things which fill us with horror. But he "errs, not knowing the Scriptures."[1] *He has no Bible.*

Let us judge charitably our Italian brother. He may seem superstitious, and lazy, and indolent, and incapable of anything great or good. But he "errs, not knowing the Scriptures." *He has no Bible.*

---

[1] Matthew 22:29.

Let us think lovingly of all Roman Catholic laymen on the Continent. We may feel disgusted by their adoring the Holy Coat of Tréves.[1] We may be shocked at their credulity about the Winking Picture of the Virgin at Rimini.[2] But we must remember that men will eat mice and rats in time of famine, and we must not marvel if souls feed on trash and garbage when priests debar them from reading the Word. They "err, not knowing the Scriptures." *They have no Bibles.*

Last of all, let us resolve to *live by the Bible more and more* every year we live. Let us resolutely take account of all our opinions and practices, of our habits and tempers, of our behaviour in public and in private, in the world, and by our own firesides. Let us measure all by the Bible, and resolve, by God's help, to conform to it. Oh! that we may learn increasingly to "cleanse our ways" by the Word! (Psalm 119:9.)

Reader, I commend all these things to your serious and prayerful attention. I want the ministers of my beloved country to be Bible-reading ministers; the congregations, Bible-reading congregations; and the nation, a Bible-reading nation. To bring about this desirable end, I cast my mite into God's treasury. The Lord grant that in your case it may prove not to have been in vain!

I remain, your affectionate friend,
J.C. RYLE.

---

[1] The Holy Coat of Tréves is a seamless garb which, according to the legend, has a miraculous capacity to grow. It was supposedly made by the Virgin Mary for the newborn Jesus, and worn by Him throughout His life—from the manger to the Passion—without alteration. Though the Bible says nothing of such a garment, and no record of it exists prior to the twelfth century, it eventually grew into an object of adoration. Since the sixteenth century, popes have paid it tribute, masses said in its honour, pilgrimages declared on its behalf, and indulgences proclaimed for those who would venerate it.

[2] The Winking Picture of the Virgin at Rimini is a picture of Mary that was given to a church at Rimini, Italy, in 1810. It manifested no signs of life until 1850, when it was seen to wink.

LIGHT FROM OLD TIMES

or
PROTESTANT
FACTS
AND MEN

J.C. RYLE

J.C. Ryle's biographical survey of the English Reformation, as
seen through the lives of men who shaped the English church.
Light extols the faith and courage of saints who went before us,
writing their names in "letters of gold," for all to see. These
pages demonstrate that Protestant liberty didn't come cheaply.
Every English-speaking Christian, who freely reads the Scriptures in his native tongue, and publicly worships God on
Sundays, owes an enormous debt to the godly giants named
here. The lives sketched in this volume, and the doctrines
uncovered by it, guide us toward the true gospel—the one
worth living for—and the one worth dying for. Hardcover, 432
pages, ISBN 0-9677603-0-5.

www.charlesnolanpublishers.com

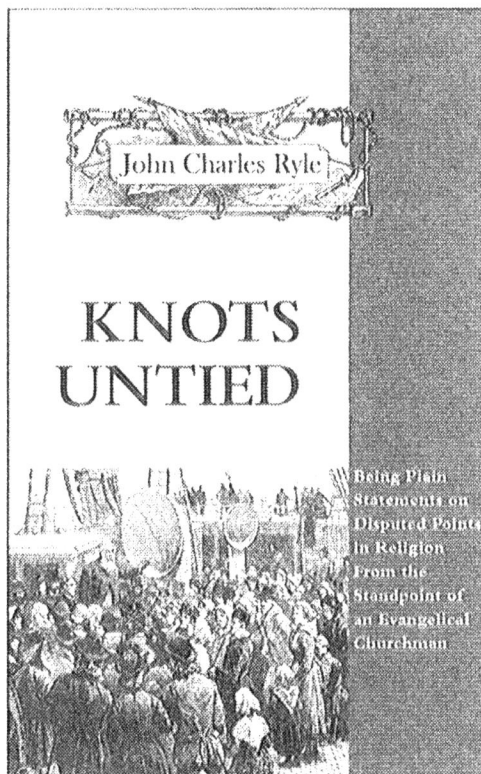

John Charles Ryle

KNOTS
UNTIED

Being Plain
Statements on
Disputed Points
in Religion
From the
Standpoint of
an Evangelical
Churchman

Writing "as a minister of Christ, a father of a family, and a lover of my country," J.C. Ryle does what he does best: make plain and understandable the seemingly difficult knots of Scripture. Evangelical truths—rich, deep, meaty truths—are here set before the hungry Christian. Food to strengthen languishing souls for the day of battle, and food to feast upon in the day of victory. "Let us have clear systematic views of the gospel of the grace of God. Nothing else will do good in the hour of sickness, in the day of trial, on the bed of death, and in the swellings of Jordan." Hardcover, 454 pages, ISBN 0-9677603-2-1.

www.charlesnolanpublishers.com

EXHORTATIONS
A CALL TO MATURITY IN WORSHIP

DOUGLAS WILSON

Pastor Douglas Wilson addresses individual Christians, the local church, and the entire body of Christ with these calls to worship. Categorized by subject, themes range from "Armies of the Living God," "Families," and "Grace," to "Reformation," "Sin," and "The Word." Each chapter begins with a prayer of adoration and ends with a prayer of confession. Pithy, provocative, and to the point, this book is suitable for private reading or family instruction. Sound, orthodox, and God-honouring, it is not seeker friendly. Like Jael, it encourages God's saints and hammers His enemies. "Wilson's words are sobering"—*The Presbyterian Witness.* Laminated hardcover, 225 pages, ISBN 0-9677603-1-3.

www.charlesnolanpublishers.com

"How Readest Thou?"
by
J.C. Ryle

Set in
11 on 13 Adobe Jenson
Composed at
Ruptüred Disc Studios, Moscow
Printed by
Jostens Printing & Publishing

Photograph of Bishop Ryle
courtesy of
Mr. Jim Wilson, Moscow

www.ingramcontent.com/pod-product-compliance
Lightning Source LLC
Chambersburg PA
CBHW072025040426

42447CB00009B/1732